Introduction

Many railway enthusiast's have questioned the claim to fame of the P class tanks of the former S.E. & C.R. "To be honest," confessed one, "this was a class which did not specially appeal to me, and I suppose I just never bothered to make the effort to photograph them on the job. On the whole I tended to dismiss the P's as a rather grotesque and generally unsuccessful Wainwright imitation of a Stroudley Terrier, and I fancy this view would have been pretty widespread during their life on the main system."

So to most during their half century on the national network they remained nonentities, tucked away in odd undistinguished corners. Like so many light-weight locomotives, they failed to match the services for which they were designed, a shortcoming one must add of most classes inevitably relegated to lighter duties as loads increased. But unlike so many other classes, the P tanks showed that same kind of resilience for survival which was a feature of the well-known Stroudley Terriers. Their tiny size and accompanying economy found them employed on duties where larger locomotives could not go or were hardly a paying proposition - sidings with sharp curvatures, coaling stage duties and light industrial railways. They remained, except for brief spells, in their natural South-Eastern habitat and were only threatened when the Kent Coast electrification eventually reached fruition,

necessitating closure o
the small Drewry dies
various wharfs and sid

Two were taken int
time the dust of the ine
of the class were in pr
lines in the South Eas
existence today is a rec
field of railway preservation. As the account will show, much hinged around the fact that when the Bluebell Railway was seeking a second Terrier for opening its train services in its first season, none was available. Southern Region came up with the offer of a P tank, and after that there was no looking back. *Bluebell* appeared to do its work as well as any Terrier, and became even more popular with the locomotive crews, as well as proving extremely economical. The Railway eventually purchased another two of the class which, in their attractive liveries, soon became endeared to the tourist public. Even the enthusiasts began to eat their words, admitting that "the last decade or so, and their resurgence in private hands and particularly 27's superb restoration to pre-1914 glory, has changed the image altogether." The P class tanks had at last stumbled upon a special niche for which they were eminently suited.

Origins and Design

Designer

The earliest suggestion concerning the construction of a new type of small tank locomotive for service with light local trains on branch lines of the South Eastern and Chatham Railway first appeared in writing in the Minutes of the Locomotive and Carriage and Wagon Sub-Committee held at Ashford Works on 4 November, 1907, indexed under "Tank Engines for Rail Cars". In attendance upon a committee top-heavy with baronets was as usual Mr. H. S. Wainwright, Locomotive, Carriage and Wagon Superintendent of the relatively new main-line Company which had been formed in 1899 as a joint Committee for two insolvent companies that had exhausted their resources through rivalry and duplication.

Harry Smith Wainwright was a Worcester man, born in 1864, who had earlier served with the Midland, the London Tilbury and Southend, and the Manchester, Sheffield and Lincolnshire Railway Companies. His father was Carriage and Wagon Superintendent of the South Eastern Railway up to 1896, and he succeeded him in that position. At the fusion of 1899, the double retirement of William Kirtley from the London Chatham and Dover Railway and of James Stirling from the S.E.R., left the way clear for the appointment of a new chief to coordinate the working of the combined Locomotive Departments, and Harry Wainwright with his proven ability already on view at Ashford was given the post which had been enlarged to take in the Carriage and Wagon Departments, an exorbitant workload which eventually led to his premature resignation through ill health in 1913. As it was, it was no light responsibility for the engines were a very mixed collection, the rails were light, the bridges required strengthening and the loading gauge was limited. Wainwright did not take long to vindicate his appointment, and under his

Harry Smith Wainwright, Locomotive, Carriage and Wagon Superintendent to the Management Committee of the SE and LCD Railways. His pronounced and clearly legible' signature was indicative of the precision and artistic design he was to bring to his workmanship. *Photo courtesy NRM York*

administration many changes were effected including the transference, completed in 1911, of the L.C.D.'s Locomotive Works at Longhedge to Ashford, enlarging the S.E.R. Works already sited there, and fitting of the L.C.D.R. stock from Westinghouse to vacuum brake to be uniform with those of the South Eastern. After completing Kirtley engines already on order, with the assistance of a first rate Chief Draughtsman in Robert Surtees, formerly at Longhedge, he launched a new series of classes starting with the dependable six-coupled C class which ran to 109 locomotives, the finely proportioned D and E class 4-4-0s and 66 medium sized H class 0-4-4 tank engines.

Not only did Wainwright intend his locomotives to perform well, but they were to look the part too, and he devised one of the most ornate and beautiful liveries ever seen in this country. This was not only to catch the public eye but, as he once stated to the Committee which was seeking to reduce the high painting costs, "I look upon the style of painting as an incentive to the men to keep their engines clean and tidy." Every engine was painted in shining green with polished dome and burnished copper cap to its chimney, and even a humble class like the P's basked in this same glory.

The Railmotors

Doubtless the idea behind such a class had been conceived earlier than the aforementioned occasion when Wainwright addressed his Committee late in 1907, stating that "he considered it advisable to have separate tank engines of suitable design for Rail Car services in any additional vehicles that may be built. He however advised that where present Railcars were doing *fairly* well, they should not be disturbed."

The "present Railcars" had been built in 1905-06 to cater more economically for passenger services on lines where either the promoters' hopes of profitable traffic had never been realised, and all the passengers could be accommodated in a single coach, or where the growing challenge of the tram required a frequent and intensive commuter service on some suburban connecting lines. A similar situation presented itself on most of the major pre-grouping railways who turned to petrol or steam rail motors. Following trials with two petrol cars (which incidentally accommodated only four passengers) on the Isle of Sheppey Light Railway early in 1904, Wainwright had plans prepared for a series of steam railmotors for which small 0-4-0 side tank units were built by Kitson & Co. Eight were built, significantly the similar number of the P tanks they preceded.

Where were the "present Railcars doing fairly well?" The initial allocation was two railmotors on the Sheppey Light Railway, two sharing the Otford-Sevenoaks and Westerham branches, two on the Hundred of Hoo branch, one on the West Wickham-Hayes and one on the Lydd-New Romney line. Within a year owing to overcrowding, Admiralty establishments and housing developments, the last three mentioned had reverted to normal services, the other lines later succumbing to P class haulage. The railmotors made spare were reallocated late in 1906 to the services between Woodside and Selsdon Road, and Strood and Chatham Central, and in July, 1907, between Hastings and Rye, Crystal Palace and Beckenham Junction, Sandling Junction and Sandgate, and in 1908 to the Dartford-Gravesend branch, all of these at one time or another later becoming P tank preserves.

The railmotors interchanged their various duties with infinite permutations, filling in here and there while one or other was inside Ashford Works for attention, so that it is difficult to trace the logic of their perambulations, and this held true to a similar extent when the P tanks arrived, often interchanging with the railcars themselves on certain duties.

Where traffic was light and tailor-made to their carrying capacity they performed adequately, if somewhat uncomfortably, but when greater demands were made upon them Wainwright soon realised their inadequacies. By and large, as D. L. Bradley emphatically states, "they were not very successful," failing to come up to expectations, most notably due to their inflexibility, hence the search for a suitable and more adaptable replacement.

Terrier Pedigree

There has been considerable debate as to how far Wainwright's P tank design was inspired by the excellent performance Stroudley's motor-fitted Terriers were giving on the Brighton system following their introduction on such workings in 1905. The issue no longer needs any qualification for, when Wainwright came to report to his Committee the introduction of the first two members of the P class, the Minutes Secretary labelled the sub-heading to this section - *"Terriers Engines Report"*, a description that must surely have been bandied about at the discussion which took place at the meeting. Indeed a close check on performance was possible since Wainwright had himself approved the purchase by the S.E.C.R. of the Terrier *Waddon* in 1904.

Unfortunately, as D. L. Bradley comments in his "Locomotives of the S.E. & C.R.", the same fine reputation achieved by the Terriers was not immediately repeated, because in the desire for economy - for his Committee were beginning to be extremely money conscious at this period to the point of authorising a nil construction of new locomotives in 1911, the P's being the last to slip through the financial net before a three year moratorium - Wainwright scaled down the dimensions to such an extent that there was often insufficient power for the work required of them, and they were found to be only slightly more successful than the railcars it had been intended that they should supersede. Though the P tank exceeded the Terrier in weight, all the principal dimensions except the initial boiler pressure of 180 lb per sq in were less.

W. G. Tilling, as well as conceding them to be designed on the lines of the Brighton Terriers, also makes the valid point that "the L.B. & S.C.R. had been using this type of engine on rail motor work for some years, but just about this time they were finding them too small and were substituting larger D class 0-4-2Ts, so Mr. Wainwright was really copying an obsolescent type, and he soon found them too small for the work for which they were intended."

This comment ties in very much with O. S. Nock's assessment that "the later stages of Wainwright's regime were less auspicious than the earlier." For some years prior to his resignation towards the close of 1913 he had been in failing health, and financial straits had reduced the S.E. & C.R. to building virtually no new locomotives. The last C had been built in 1908, the last programmed H appeared in 1910 and no new express engine had been constructed since 1909, all classes designed some years earlier, and somehow the initial enthusiasm of the new Company had waned. An unsatisfactory state of affairs existed in the nerve centre of Ashford Works where the shortcomings of the Locomotive Department received a barrage of complaints from many quarters. Sheer overwork was taking toll of Wainwright's health, but a contributory cause may have been related to his own personality. He was a carriage and wagon man by training, "more of an

The engine unit for Steam Motor No. 1, constructed at Ashford in 1905, and assigned to the Sheppey Light Railway services.
Photo courtesy NRM York

Railcar No. 2, which entered traffic in February 1905, was sent to work the Toomer Loop between Strood and Chatham Central where the entire station staff appear to have turned out to be photographed on this occasion. Of added interest, beside the longitudinal sleepers, is the ballast between tracks to catch stray cinders from setting the timber viaduct alight.   *J. Minnis collection*

When the independent Sheppey Light Railway became the responsibility of the SECR, Wainwright was quick to secure the purchase of redundant Stroudley Terrier No. 654 *Waddon* of 1876 from the LB&SCR, the handover taking place at Hastings. It was equipped with vacuum ejectors, painted Brunswick green and renumbered 751. Known patronisingly as *Little Tich*, it went on to serve in numerous small corners of the SECR empire on motor trains, as works and harbour shunter and as shed pilot, taking turn and turn about across the whole gamut of P class duties. It eventually retired from Lancing Works to be presented to the Canadian Historical Association on 4 June 1962.
Author's collection

artist than an engineer", and never a strong administrator.

However in locomotive design in profitable partnership with Robert Surtees he produced locomotive creations of outstanding beauty by which he will always be remembered. The detailed locomotive design was sound and the workmanship put into the engines was evident from the longevity of the S.E. & C.R. classes built in the first decade of the century, and indeed in the case of the P tanks by their continuing usefulness even today.

Construction

Preliminary drawings for the class appear to have been ready by the start of 1908, for on 25 January, Wainwright was able to dispatch a letter with the outline design of the small six-wheeled coupled engine for working either cars or ordinary carriages, and suggesting tenders be invited. Bradley states that Wainwright had originally intended Ashford to undertake the work, but in the intervening time, pressure of repairs had forced him to approach the Locomotive Committee for authority to transfer the construction to a private manufacturer. Meanwhile there were still some details to complete, for on 3 February, in early reply to a query by Surtees from Ashford, Wainwright replied:- "Yes, the engine is to be fitted with steam heating apparatus." On 12 February he was back to his Committee with drawings prepared by the Locomotive Engineer, and intimated he could now undertake erection of the engines at Ashford Works, the cost to be debited to the capital account. The change of mind arose because the lowest tender, by the Vulcan Foundry topped £2000 compared with Ashford's estimate of £1,480. Accordingly, Wainwright was instructed to rearrange his repair schedules to permit assembly at Ashford, overtime and weekend working to be introduced if necessary to ensure punctual delivery. He wrote to Surtees a week later reporting the favourable decision of the Management Committee and requesting, "Please have the necessary drawings completed as quickly as possible, and have the material ordered." Next day, 20 February, J. Masterton,

Locomotive Shops Manager at Ashford, wrote from the Foundry, "I shall be glad to have the drawings for all steel casting cylinders and boilers soon, so that the pattern work for the above may be pushed on." Things were moving at last but the delays proved fortuitous for according to Bradley they presented Wainwright with the opportunity of revising the design in the light of more recent information. Dimensions were increased and various minor modifications made, which raised the cost to £1,740 each.

Design

The first two members of the class, Nos. 753 and 754, emerged from Ashford Works on 18 and 23 February, 1909, respectively, and brief trials were held on the New Romney branch, the usual venue for running in, but the first the world at large was to hear about them appeared in print in the railway periodicals for May. The largest splash was in "The Locomotive" of 15 May, which sallied forth in the inimitable patronising style of that period to the effect that "We are indebted to Mr. Harry S. Wainwright, the chief locomotive engineer, for the accompanying illustration of a new type of small tank locomotive known as Class P, which have recently been constructed at Ashford for service with light local trains on branch lines." It spoke of the design as "compact" and went on to give the leading dimensions.

"The Railway Magazine" reproduced only the photograph of 754 and featured the chief details in an extended caption.

The leading dimensions of this "new class of small 0-6-0T type" were as follows:-

Cylinders 12 in. diameter by 18 in. stroke

Couple wheels	3ft. 9 ½ in.
Wheelbase	11ft. 0 in.
Boiler diameter	3ft. 3⅛ in.
Boiler length	7ft. 7 ½ in.
Firebox length	3 ft. 10 in.
Grate area	9.1 sq. ft.

Heating surfaces -	Tubes	387.34 sq. ft.
	Firebox	51.69 sq. ft.

	Total	439.03 sq. ft.

Capacity of Coal Bunker 18 cwt.
Capacity of Water Tank 550 gallons
   Working pressure 180 lb. per sq. in.

Weight in working order:
On leading coupled wheels	9 tons 0 cwt.
On driving coupled wheels	9 tons 10 cwt.
On trailing coupled wheels	10 tons 0 cwt.

Total	28 tons 10 cwt.

All the locomotives were fitted with Stone's Patent Louvre spark arrester, Furness lubricators on the smokebox sides, carriage heating and steam sanding apparatus, Stirling reversing gear and automatic vacuum brake, two No 6 Gresham injectors and leaf springs to all wheels. The cylinders were inclined at 1 in 9 with 2ft. 3 in. centres and the valve chest between, while reversing was by lever. Some were later fitted for motor training working with the wire, rod and pulley system. At first the reversing cylinders were sited within the cabs, but at the footplatemen's request were later resited on the leading end of the right-hand side tank in order to give more elbow room and keep the cabs cooler in hot weather.

The standard "pagoda" type cab, such a distinctive feature of Wainwright's tank engines, was fitted to the class. On such a diminutive locomotive it appeared excessively tall and, following the first two pioneer members, the rest of the class was turned out with roofs several inches lower. The roof also embodied the "lip" familiar to all Wainwright's tank engines, designed to throw the rain water well clear of the driver's head as he peered over the side of the cab.

Livery

All entered traffic resplendent in the elaborately lined-out Wainwright livery used on all classes of S.E. & C.R. locomotives. The P class were painted in gleaming dark Brunswick green, lined out by lighter green bands edged with red and yellow lines. Raised brass numerals were attached to the bunkerside, while on the tank sides appeared the Railway's attractive coat-of-arms, above which were inscribed the Railway's initials. Burnished brass was used for the dome covers, boiler mountings, the Ramsbottom safety valves, window surrounds and beading on the mini-splashers above the leading wheels, while the graceful chimneys were surmounted by copper caps. The frames were painted a reddish-brown colour often quoted variously as maroon or vermilion. Large yellow numerals were applied to the buffer beams.

Numbering Problems

The dispersed numbering of the class was of course due to the S.E. & C.R. policy of slotting in newly constructed engines into gaps left by withdrawal of older ones. 753 and 754 were however viewed as additions, not renewals, and assumed the next new numbers on the Locomotive list, the highest until the arrival of the L class in 1914. But the further order for six more caused some headaches in the Locomotive Department, worth relating in some detail.

Responsible in part was the rigid archaic renewal system employed by the Company at this stringent period of only building a new engine provided it replaced a withdrawn one, on a one to one basis. Mention of the further batch of six had been minuted on 28 July, 1909: "9 old engines to be replaced by 9 tank engines to be built at Ashford on Renewal Account during the current half-year." A suggestion had been put forward that the 6 small six-wheeled coupled engines authorised on 23 June at an estimate of £1300 each on Capital Account, should be part of the renewals. Wainwright, however, proposed that the arrangements already made for the present half-year should stand, and that next half-year the 6 small with 3 of the larger H tanks should be charged to Renewal Account.

But which six locomotives the P's were to replace had been taxing Wainwright the previous summer. Mr. Barber of Longhedge Works had replied on 14 September, 1908: "I have gone into this matter and find it of some difficulty to determine which class of engines it would be advisable to replace. Am sending particulars of M class 616-621." Kirtley had introduced these 4-4-0s in 1877, and large amounts had been expended upon them during the past five years. They were not fitted with vacuum brakes but their boilers had been renewed comparatively recently. Surtees commented: "Seeing the large amount that has been spent on these engines in recent years and there is the question of working Westinghouse main line trains to be considered, I would suggest these engines be kept running for a few more years. I would call attention to the Radial tank engines of class D, 554-559, six engines built in 1873. These I think could well be replaced." The engines mentioned were Martley's "Large Scotchmen" 0-4-2 well tanks concerning which relevant details were supplied from Longhedge a week later indicating the last firebox-boiler renewals between 1901-3, and details of average annual expenditure only slightly below the M class. Again to Mr. Surtees for remarks, who replied on the back of the letter: "I would suggest that these tank engines be renewed in preference to the M class - these engines (the D's) are on the Herne Hill and Holborn, Nunhead and Greenwich, and Sheppey Railway service. They are fitted with Westinghouse and Vacuum brakes and could they (the H's) work these services? Please ask Battersea Running Dept."

G. Bennett of Battersea replied on 25 September indicating general agreement but misgivings at the suggestion of replacing his D class workings with H class engines, the latter vacuum only while several suburban trains were fitted with Westinghouse only, adding, "I am short of tank engines, having to wash engines out at night so as to cover the traffic during the day," and concluding that it would be difficult but the D's could very well be replaced. On 28 September, 1908, L. Daniel of the Locomotive, Carriage and Wagon Department at Ashford came down decisively, as it proved, with this advice. The Herne Hill-Holborn service could well be covered by three R class tanks presently based at Bricklayers Arms. "It is impossible to do away with the D class tank engines until more vacuum stock is provided. I certainly think that if possible the D tanks should be renewed."

So the class lingered on to "be broken up as they come into the shops," but at the start of 1911 556/7/9 were still in traffic, the latter two at Sheerness, only being transferred to the Supplementary List at the end of that year. The additional six P tanks had meanwhile entered service, and from the reproduced letter of 14 January, 1910, it will be seen that the first four numbers were taken from withdrawn members of the Q class, and only the final two from the D Radial Tanks. The P tanks, however, can well be considered their legal heirs, taking over D turns on the Greenwich Park and Sheppey services and eventually assuming four of their numbers.

The Auto-Train Services

The Pioneer Pair

The first two members of the class, Nos. 753 and 754, had been ordered at a Locomotive Committee meeting on 23 January, 1908, at an estimated cost of £1480 each. On 27 March, 1909, Harry Wainwright was able to report to his Committee on his so-called "Terrier Engines". "With reference to the two small six-wheeled Tank engines authorised to be built at Ashford, both engines had been put into service and were working in a highly successful manner - one between Reading and Ash, and the other on the Otford service." Both locomotives had entered service the previous month, no evidence regarding which entered service first having as yet come to light, though 754 was chosen for the official photograph.

The Otford Shuttle

After a short period of trials on the New Romney branch, 753 went to Tonbridge shed and ran up daily to Sevenoaks to work the shuttle service from Tubs Hill to the bay platform at Otford, a working that became a virtual P tank monopoly from the beginning until 1926. This humble by-way began as an alternative route to Dover, a 9 mile single track branch of the nominally independent Sevenoaks Railway from Sevenoaks Junction (later renamed Swanley) to Bat and Ball on the outskirts of Sevenoaks. Backed by the L.C.D.R. it opened in 1862, and after overcoming the opposition of local landlords, the temporary and inconvenient site of the southern terminus was extended through to the S.E.R. Tubs Hill station in 1869.

Above: The first pair of P tanks emerged from Ashford Works in February 1909 as Nos. 753/4. However it was the latter that was used for the official photograph, endowed with full Wainwright livery and pagoda cab. It was immediately allocated for working the Reading-Ash and Aldershot Town motor train services.
Author's collection

Left: After brief trials, No. 753 was despatched to Tonbridge shed for the Sevenoaks to Otford services. October 1909 found it employed running trials on a selection of branches including the Westerham line, following which the Management Committee were suitably enough impressed to give orders for another six to be constructed. The cleaning gang at Tonbridge were proud enough of their new little steed to have their picture taken with this latest addition to their stud.
Photo courtesy NRM York

In 1874 a new line was opened to Maidstone from a junction on it near Otford, and a southern spur was added to enable through running from Sevenoaks to Maidstone in 1880. Two years later a station about half a mile north of the triangular junction was opened adjoining the road at Otford where by the end of 1901 a bay platform was put in to work the service from Sevenoaks.

After the union of 1899 the original arrangement of trains running direct to Maidstone was revived, and the Sevenoaks line quickly came to be regarded as an appendix to the Swanley Junction - Maidstone route, and it was this infrequent shuttle service that the P class took over in 1909. Doubtless they availed themselves of coal and water at the little sub-shed at Bat and Ball which was not taken out of use until as late as 1935 after the line had been electrified, though a small coal stage was also provided and staffed at Tubs Hill. The engines would have returned to base at Tonbridge for boiler washout and maintenance.

The Reading-Ash-Aldershot Motor Services

754 was allocated to Reading shed, that western outpost of the S.E. & C.R. The origins of this extended arm are admirably covered in R. W. Kidner's booklet on "The Reading to Tonbridge Line." As part of the infighting to tap the vast military traffic of the area the S.E.R. sought powers to gain access to Aldershot, the key centre, and in 1879 was able to lay in a connection named Aldershot Town Junction just south of the point where its line passed under the L.S.W. route from Pirbright Junction to Farnham. The South Eastern was given running powers in return for similar powers for the L.S.W.R. between Ash Junction and North Camp, the latter in fact never invoked. Thus South-Eastern trains were enabled to run into Aldershot Town and South Camp, as the L.S.W.R. station was then named, without reversal at Farnham, and after a number of variations a shuttle service between Aldershot and Ash, together with some through trains, became an established part of the timetable. It added a new dimension to services at this point with 11 Up and 12 Down trains. Quite a number did not connect with any 'main line' train at Ash, and Kidner concludes that "the generous service was one more example of railway's usually fatal desire to run a local train service."

With the thickening up of military traffic in the Camberley area it was decided at the end of February, 1909, to introduce a motor service over the Reading-Ash section, and Sandhurst Halt was opened in that year, followed by the new Sindlesham and Hurst Halt (later Winnersh Halt) on the first day of March, 1910, by which time 178 had been placed in service and sent to assist 754. Ash station has two bay platforms facing north. One bay would have sufficed for the Aldershot shuttle, but the motor service from Reading necessitated a second bay and additionally enabled interchange of sets and engines to return to base at Reading, for only one engine was sub-shedded at Ash. On Mondays to Fridays there were 4 trains daily (5 on Saturdays and none on Sundays) which ran from Reading to Ash, then reversed to intensify the service on the shuttle to Aldershot. Between the latter two points trains carried square white boards with one horizontal black bar on both left and right irons, at night a green lamp left and a white right. For through trains on arrival at Ash from Aldershot the green lamp was removed.

A small single road locomotive sub-shed, (still intact and in use as a store quite recently) administered from Reading,

lay beside the Down side bay, and it was here that 754 and, one of the two P tanks later allocated to Reading was subshedded and serviced. The purpose of the arrival a year later, of 178 was to take over the running of the Aldershot shuttle from Q class 0-4-4Ts. The Reading-Ash motor service died with the War when military traffic increased out of all proportion beyond the capacity of the auto-sets, and the two P class representatives at that period, 27 and 754 answered wartime calls and moved to other spheres. The Aldershot shuttle continued in other hands until the Guildford-Aldershot electrification on 1 January 1939.

Six More Ordered

The performance of the first two members of the class was apparently such as to warrant further additions. On 23 June, 1909, at London Bridge the Management Committee reported under the heading - "Small Engines - 6 to be built at Ashford for use in local services" and minuted under "Terrier Engines" stated: "The two small 6 wheel coupled engines authorised to be built at Ashford in Feb. 1908, are working with excellent results between Reading and Ash, and Sevenoaks and Otford respectively, and the General Manager (Mr. Vincent W. Hill) suggests that 6 similar locomotives should be provided for use in the undermentioned services - Crowhurst and Bexhill, Paddock Wood and Maidstone, Strood and New Brompton, Birchington and Ramsgate Harbour, Norwood and Beckenham. The Locomotive Superintendent estimates cost of engines if built at Ashford at £1300, but he cannot promise complete construction under 12 months." This Wainwright in fact achieved timewise, though a later estimate raised the cost to £1835 each. The construction of the class came to be an exact replica in building pattern to that of the railcars where the first two had entered service at the beginning of 1905 and a further six had followed between March and June, 1906.

This was an ambitious programme for the class as regards services. The Thanet one was the only one that became a permanent fixture as far as the P class were concerned. This with the Strood and the Beckenham services are already railmotor preserves. Of interest is the Paddock Wood-Maidstone proposition, the result of a memorial from the inhabitants of that district submitted in December, 1908, to which the Committee agreed in principle to the suggested running of a motor train service, constructing new Halts worked by short trains, independent of ordinary services, drawn by one or more of the small six-wheeled tank engines to be built at Ashford. But in the event the commitment was not followed through. However in October 1909, 753 was temporarily taken off its Otford shuttle to run trials between Nunhead and Greenwich Park, Beckenham Junction and Norwood Junction, Chatham Central and Strood and over the Westerham branch.

So it was that construction was confirmed in a memo of the Locomotive, Carriage and Wagon Sub-Committee at a meeting at London Bridge on 2 March, 1910, regarding renewals in the half year to 30 June, 1910, noting "6 old engines to be replaced by 6 small six wheels coupled engines." The building dates for these were as follows: 27 and 178 in February, 1910, 323 in April, 325 in May, and 555 and 558 in June. Incidentally, 323 was actually completed and ran trials on 26 April, but was then stored in the paint shop until 16 July, while 325 similarly spent the period 7 May to 20 July, 1910, in store. This may well have been to await fitting auto gear as initially Ashford was a little tardy in fitting up the later members of the class, or to await the Board's decision concerning livery. Bradley mentions that during this period

323 was experimentally painted lake to match a motor train equipped carriage set, while 325 was paired with three carriages painted Brunswick green. These changes in livery failed to please the directors and both engines entered traffic in the Company's standard livery. All six were equipped with steam reversing and the cab height was lowered by 4 ½ in. compared with the pioneer pair. Two, however, were designated light passenger engines and were not therefore immediately equipped for motor train operation.

The Sheppey Light Railway

It was 27 which went to the Isle of Sheppey Light Railway, displacing "Little Tich" which had been much liked by the Sheerness shed men. The latter, 751, was the former Stroudley Terrier *Waddon*, purchased from the L.B. & S.C.R. in 1904 for the Sheppey Light Railway goods services and as a back up to the passenger-carrying Railmotor No. 1 which uniquely carried the inscription "Sheppey Light Railway." After sterling service there the Terrier's boiler was condemned in October, 1909, and a replacement could not be supplied till the New Year. Because of the delay the latest P tank was despatched, and despite several attempts by Sheerness shed to obtain its return, 751 was sent to the London area. It had a colourful further career, filling in for the P tanks when one was away at Ashford for repairs, making recorded appearances at Sandgate and Richborough. For some time after it paralleled the fortunes of the P class and today stands preserved in Canada.

The Sheppey Light Railway scheme originated in 1896 when Mr. H. F. (later Colonel) Stephens, the famous light railway engineer, was invited by a local landowner, Lord Harris, to report on the feasibility of a line to serve the villages on the Isle of Sheppey. After a site visit in May, 1897, a scheme was drawn up for presentation to the Light Railway Commissioners, and the Light Railway Order was granted in May, 1899. Construction began immediately, the contract being awarded to W.Rigby (a friend of Stephens) at a total cost, including land, of £43,000. Stations were constructed in Stephens' familiar corrugated iron style and many of the platforms were of simple construction with sleeper facings; the line was lightly laid with 64 lb rail, there were no bridges and the eight intersections with public roads were made by level crossings. As an economy measure Stephens proposed that passenger trains of up to three vehicles would not be required to be fitted with continuous brakes, but this did not find favour with the authorities.

The Sheppey line was opened in August, 1901, worked at the outset by the S.E. & C.R. and Stephens had no further involvement with it. It was a speculative line, ostensibly justified by existing potential traffic, and built in the hope that Leysdown would become a popular resort and residential centre. It linked with the Sheerness branch at Queenborough, 8 ¾ miles away across a bleak wilderness of marshy meadows and desolate wastes. It was a cheap line with a summit of just under 100 ft. above sea level, gently undulating grades and the slightest of earthworks. The S.E. & C.R. which had leased the line, expressed sufficient faith to buy it in 1905 and introduced a service of seven weekday trains, five of which had London connections at Queenborough, using 751 hauling three former L.C.D.R. four wheeled coaches with the compartments connected to vestibules, and a pair of railmotors. Farm sidings at Brambledown and Harty Road were upgraded to halts. After 27's arrival at Sheerness, railmotors still made appearances until 1912 when 27 also bowed out and P class workings remain unrecorded until the 1923 Grouping.

The Gravesend West Branch

As mentioned previously, 178, allocated to Reading, went to Ash to supplement 754 on the shuttle to Aldershot. The fifth member of the class broke new ground, 323 going to Orpington shed to work with Gravesend West branch at first using conventional stock. Opened on 10 May 1886 by the L.C.D.R. following its takeover of the nominally independent Gravesend Railway Company, the branch left the Rochester main line at Fawkham Junction half a mile west of Fawkham station, and ran along five miles of double track to Gravesend (West Street) beyond which a 7 chain extension led on to the West Pier. It was doomed to mediocrity from the outset, not only through the S.E.R.'s shorter and less difficult route from Charing Cross (24 miles as opposed to 27 ½ from Victoria), but also from the competition of the London Tilbury and Southend's cheap through fares via the Tilbury Ferry. After the First World War the Rotterdam Boat Train service was moved over the Tilbury Docks, reducing the Gravesend West branch to a purely local affair. The only other attraction on the branch, the pleasure resort of Rosherville Gardens adjoining to which a halt had been specially opened, closed in 1910. Thus when the P class took over the branch passenger workings, the volume of traffic was already much reduced from earlier days. Traffic dwindled and not even the 1939 electrification of the main line availed and the passenger services ceased on 3 August 1954, and goods by virtue of sidings links to the Northfleet paper mills and APCM cement works lingered on until 1968.

The branch service started from Swanley Junction where, following departure of the main line train, the Gravesend auto train would draw out of the standing siding at the Up end. The service soon came to be worked by push-pull sets with the engine at the Down end, and water was almost invariably taken on the Down side platform end, and conveniently opposite was a coal stage cut into the bank for the branch engine's use. The service of trains per weekday was handled chiefly by 323 up to the middle period of the war, then by 558 released through the closure of the Greenwich Park branch, 753 was there in February 1919, and P tank haulage continued until the R class assumed the services just prior to the Grouping.

The Beckenham-Norwood Shuttle

The other Orpington P turn was the working of the Beckenham Junction to Norwood Junction service, a useful but lightly patronised outer suburban link between the SECR and LBSCR trunk routes. 1910 was the first year on which the P class appeared regularly on the service, 323 having a brief spell in September and taking over when required from Terrier 751. The latter was itself employed at various locations as a relief for railcars or P class tanks away for repair at Ashford. The same pattern was used in 1913 (when 178 was photographed on the service), and again in 1915 with 751 bearing the lion's share. The service ran at intervals, and to avoid running down to replenish coal at Orpington a small coal stage was provided at Beckenham Junction.

The scene at Beckenham Junction in August 1913 with No. 178 lingering in the half shadows with the shuttle service to Norwood formed by the single LCDR coach No. 2101. A connecting train is unloaded in the bay platform.   *H.J.P. Rutherford Collection/NRM York*

The Greenwich Park Branch

The next two of the class, 325 and 555, prior to their teaming up on the Greenwich Park branch, were allocated to Ashford and New Brompton (later Gillingham) respectively. 325 was most probably used on the Sandling Junction-Sandgate branch and 555 worked the Chatham Central-Strood services via the Toomer loop line until the latter's closure on 30 September 1911. On 17 April 1912 the Locomotive Committee authorised expenditure of £244 to fit two P class engines and four L.C.D.R. bogie carriages with motor train equipment. 325 was given the necessary gear and with 555 opened the new services between Nunhead and Greenwich Park.

This former L.C.D.R. project had sought to tap the South Eastern's virtual monopoly of the North Kent suburban traffic, and aimed at Woolwich. It left the main line at Nunhead, and the two miles to Blackheath Hill via Brockley Lane and Lewisham Road stations were opened in 1871, the remaining half mile to Greenwich only coming in 1888. It enjoyed an intensive service of 26 trains a day to counter the growing threat of the tramcar, but basically it was a lost cause since it merely skirted the southern approaches to the City compared with the direct S.E.R. route.

The P tanks with their auto-trains took over the workings, and also some of the numbers, from Martley's D class 0-4-2Ts with their assortment of four and six wheel coaches necessitating running round at each end. The branch locomotives were based at Longhedge where the allocation in July 1914, of 178, 555 and 558 covered the ex L.C.D.R.'s "South London" line Victoria - St Pauls service, and to Greenwich Park from both Nunhead and Victoria, and some of the services to Crystal Palace (High Level) which also came off the main line at Nunhead.

A very poor photograph exists showing 555 at Nunhead on a Crystal Palace working. Apart from the Crystal Palace itself the line had little attraction, since it not only paralleled the LBSC main line but also duplicated stations at Honor Oak and Lordship Lane. Both branches from Nunhead were wartime casualties, closing on the first day of 1917, but the Crystal Palace line reopened on 1 March 1919, served from Orpington shed until electrified in 1925, repeating its wartime closure experience in May 1944 and yet again reopening in March 1946, some ten years after the Palace had gone up in flames, and finally closed in September 1954, too early to be saved by the proposed new Sports Centre. The Greenwich Park branch lingered on as a store for outworn coaching stock till abandoned in 1929 except for the westernmost part which, by building a ramp down from the point where the branch crossed the former South Eastern line south at St. Johns, was used as a loop line for cross-London freight workings and, later, passenger services to reach Hither Green.

No. 325 at Greenwich Park in July 1912 has its polished chimney cap and dome cover painted over. The class was equipped with Furness lubricators on the smokebox sides, steam sanding, carriage heating, Stones patent louvre spark arrester, two No. 6 Gresham injectors and leaf springs to all wheels. *LPC/IAL*

Services in Thanet

558, the last member of the class went to Margate West shed to work the local service between Birchington and Ramsgate Sands. A set of stations in close proximity spanned a group of very popular and fashionable Kentish holiday resorts requiring a local service to supplement the long distance ones in the area. These ran at odd times during the day but in the summer months were filled to capacity so that the standby railmotor was often in use. 558 was the last to be motor-train equipped in December 1912, and was then posted to Tonbridge.

Soon after the outbreak of war 178 took over these workings, and later during the war 323 and 754 were sent to Margate, the second engine to work the Margate Sands-Minster service which included reversal at the old Ramsgate Town station. In 1919 555 arrived to supplement the Minster services which were extended to Canterbury West in the early morning and evening, a shortlived service which failed to catch on with the local populace and was withdrawn in September 1919, when, deserted by its colleagues, 555 remained to become the Margate shed pilot.

The Westerham Branch

753 which appears to have made Tonbridge its permanent home up to the war, was joined there at the end of 1912 by newly motor-fitted 558, and this enabled a member of the class there to work the Westerham branch services, a 4¾ mile single track route running below the scarp of the North Downs from Dunton Green through Brasted to Westerham. It was opened independently in 1881 and immediately invested in the S.E.R. The service topped over a dozen trains each way on weekdays when a pair of railmotors got in on the act in 1906 with a new halt at Chevening and Westerham's little sub-shed whose parent depot was Tonbridge closed down, though the ashpit was retained and the locomotives could still coal up there. However there was apparently more traffic on the branch than the authorities had realised, and a tail load of an added six-wheeled coach proved an operational liability, so late in 1910 the line reverted to Q class operation with three-coach sets. It was this situation that set Harry

Wainwright's mind posing how costs might be reduced, and to produce in the P tanks a very economical solution.

By 1914 558 had been exchanged for 325, but once again traffic ran ahead of capacity and the persistent Q class 0-4-4Ts once again took over. In the early 'twenties 178 and 323, fitted with a modified auto-train gear and hauling a three-coach set, resumed taking turns when spared from the Otford line till 1926 when the class was phased out as a passenger locomotive.

Motor Working Stock

To work with the P class the Company authorised early in 1912 two 2-coach bogie auto sets Nos. 271/2 to be converted from LCDR main line bogie vehicles. These started life sandwiching the P tanks, one on each side of the engine. One trailer car contained a driver's compartment and seven Third class compartments, the other was a driving composite of three Seconds and three Firsts. The locomotive could be driven from either end of the train, the driver's compartment being fitted with a regulator handle, brake valve, hand brake and a communication cord to the whistle. The sets first worked the Greenwich Park branch, transferring to the Ash-Aldershot shuttle as orthodox two-coach sets when the former closed in 1917, and ended their days there in the early 'thirties.

On the other workings, sets of three-coach LCDR four wheelers, referred to later, ended their days on the Westerham and Gravesend West services. Another conversion available for single coach working was the LCDR six wheeled carriage No. 2101 which, as Bradley recalls, was turned "into a motor train trailer with guard, luggage and driving sections, and accommodation for 40 third class passengers in four compartments." Though generally the preserve of SECR Terrier 751 on the Beckenham Junction to Norwood Junction shuttle, it appears to have been used partnered to P tanks when on that duty.

One snag to the motor train arrangement occurred when taking water from platform columns. For instance at Westerham the water column was situated by the site of the former engine shed and, when it was necessary to take water, engine and coaches shunted from the platform once the passengers had all alighted, and back again after accomplishing the manoeuvre in time to work the next train out.

Difficulties arose where motor sets of three of four carriages had to be worked on lines where traffic exceeded initial expectations, and these increases proved beyond the capacity of the small boiler and power of the P class. This contributed to the removal of the gear from some of the class which briefly returned to workings with conventional stock or shed pilot duties. Between December 1912 and July 1913, 178, 323, 556 and 754 had their auto gear modified by Ashford Works for service with a number of recently converted motor coach sets, Nos. 266-270, 273-4.

At this period not only were members of the class frequently changed around following Works visits but the auto-train gear was removed and refitted in the modified form to no logical pattern. Indeed 558 was not motor train equipped until December 1912 when it went to Tonbridge to serve the Westerham branch. The outbreak of the Great War found the class disposed as follows: 27 and 754, Reading and Ash; 178, 555 and 558 at Battersea for various services from Nunhead; 323 at Orpington for the Swanley - Gravesend West Street turns; and 325 and 753 at Tonbridge for the Otford and Westerham services.

First World War Duties

The S.E. & C.R. War Effort

The outbreak of the 1914-1918 war turned the S.E. & C.R. into a front line railway by virtue of its close proximity to France. Featuring "the S.E. & C.R. in the Great War" in the Railway and Travel Monthly of August, 1918, "G. A. Sekon" writes: "The geographical position of the S.E. & C.R. system makes it of paramount importance in the conveyance of men and materials for our Army and Navy during the stress of War conditions. Luckily the S.E. & C.R., being an amalgamation of two at one time extremely competitive systems, is blessed with two or more routes to all the important places it serves."

It bore the brunt of transporting the B.E.F. across the Channel in 1914, and subsequently of fresh troops in their thousands for the whole duration of the War. Troop trains, ambulance trains, leave trains were integrated into the web of normal services, but it was not only a question of moving men. The far bulkier loads of materials, supplies, vehicle reinforcements were greatly in excess of what the basically carrying "Channel Packet" ports of Dover and Folkestone could manage. Besides the S.E. & C.R. also dealt with the bulk of material required to establish the great supply base at Boulogne.

No. 555 shunting in the Stores Yard at Richborough on 8 September 1916. Over in the right background, a squad of troops are marched back to their tented headquarters after a turn of duty moving stores. Walls of boxes stand in the centre of the photograph, awaiting transport across the Channel. *Photo courtesy Imperial War Museum*

Richborough Port

The Government therefore quickly decided with some urgency to revive the ancient port of Richborough which lay on the estuary of the Stour below Sandwich. The Richborough undertaking and its inception was the brain-child of the Inland Waterways and Docks Division at the War Office. An Inland Water Transport Section of the Royal Engineers was formed in December 1914 to operate and develop transport on the canals and waterways of Northern France and Belgium, and chose to develop their base at Richborough using an additional area covering 2200 acres, formerly marsh grazing lands by the mouth of the Stour. The area was taken over by the War Office, and extensive sidings comprising about 60 miles of standard gauge track were laid down from the redeveloped harbour to the South Eastern's line between Minster and Sandwich, the connection facing Minster on the Down (east) side of the line. Alas, for its future well-being, the East Kent Railway's extension proposals of 1910 had not closed the gap soon enough to gain the war traffic that came to Richborough, belatedly completing a goods only connection from Eastry which continued until 27 October 1949. The R.O.D. took over the Old Wharf, laid immediate plans for a new one to accommodate train ferries and was responsible for shunting the larger sidings. The connecting spur to the Canterbury line was laid in at once.

It was known when first opened in 1916 as 'Richborough Siding', being used for goods traffic on War Office account, and in March 1917 as 'Richborough Wharf'. A new exchange yard there was opened on 14 May 1917. A special train was to run to and fro from the temporary Richborough Military Halt to connect with normal S.E & C.R. services.

The most important development in facilities for dealing with the heavy military stores traffic to and from the Continent was the construction of extensive works there for the purpose of trans-Channel train ferry and barge service. Construction of the new Richborough embarkation wharf commenced in June, 1916, and progressed so well that a regular service of barges was in operation by December, 1916, and continued till the Armistice. The train ferry, whose terminal was on the north side of the river almost at the point where it becomes Pegwell Bay, came into existence in January, 1917, Calais and Dunkirk being equipped with corresponding terminal facilities. Just over a year later the train ferry to Calais commenced regular operation on 10 February, 1918. Loads carried included locomotives taken over on their own wheels.

555 was sent up to act as Richborough yard pilot during this period of intense activity when the new wharf and train ferry terminal were being constructed. The capacity of the train ferry berth with eight cranes was reckoned as about 500 tons daily with single shift, or 1000 tons daily with double shift. The P class was considered more suitable than the larger R.O.D. locomotives available for working onto the ferries, for loading and unloading once the ferry was operative, and the Traffic Superintendent at Richborough was to requisition one day's engine power ahead from the CME at Ashford who was to provide locomotive staff. Two P class engines worked the wharf, as nothing heavier was allowed over the connecting line, part of a total of ten locomotives in steam every day. 555 was joined by 558 which seems to have spent most of the period of hostilities fulfilling this vital role, apart from March-April, 1916, when it had to go to Ashford

for a replacement copper tube plate, and Maunsell sent Terrier 751 to Richborough to help out until the P returned. Meanwhile 555 enjoyed a break in the summer and autumn of 1916 acting as Redhill station pilot, in September filling in at Reading and Ash, and in November working the Sandgate branch, opened in 1874 from a junction on the main Ashford-Dover line via Hythe to Sandgate, only three mile distant from Folkestone Harbour. In 1888 a new station called Sandling, with separate platforms on the branch was opened at the junction. Wartime traffic in an area where many service personnel were billeted caused Ashford based P tanks, 325 and 555 which were allocated there in 1917, to take over for a period from the railmotors, few of which saw any service after this date.

Early in 1919 control of the port was handed over to the SECR who became an Agent of the War Office in dealing with traffic, dredging, working and repair of barges, and similarly for the train ferry. 555 returned to Richborough to rejoin 558 which departed for Orpington, but was soon back with its former companion and both were still busy in the spring of 1919 coping with the return flow of military traffic, carriages

as well as locomotives. A picture in the March, 1919, issue of "Railway and Travel Monthly" shows the Channel Ferry end on to the Landing stage at Richborough with two unidentifiable P tanks in view. Richborough Port's contribution to the war effort was staggering. 1,257,545 dead-weight tons of war material were despatched, 4000 bargeloads of ammunition for which specials were run from the powder works at Faversham, 784,741 tons of guns and ordnance stores, 70,877 tons of Army Service Corps supplies. The Ferry load figures were two million tons of war materials, 19,818 trucks and locomotives and 734 tanks. All too suddenly the intense activity of the wartime port subsided as quickly as it came, and silting up, the redundant harbour soon lay neglected, the sidings becoming a large rusty expanse of knitted trackwork, coal for the new power station at Richborough coming direct from Betteshanger colliery via SECR metals. With the abandonment of the ferry service in 1920, the P tanks, similarly out of work, found themselves back at Margate West shed that same year. The Richborough complex was however reactivated in the Second World War but the War Department used its own locomotives.

Another member of the class, number screened by the military clad shunter on the cab steps, operates in the Train Ferries Section at Richborough on 23 June 1917. The revetment and construction work in the foreground must have been good preparation for the real thing in the trenches. *Photo courtesy Imperial War Museum*

Service Overseas

The SECR was operating at full stretch throughout the war and its locomotive resources were so fully committed that relatively few demands were made upon its stock by the Railway Operating Division, and only twelve locomotives saw service across the Channel. The record needs setting straight in respect of N.Wakeman's SECR Locomotive List published by the Oakwood Press, where six of the P class are mentioned as operating in France with the R.O.D. In fact only two of the class, 27 and 753, were shipped over to France and at an earlier period of shorter duration. This is confirmed in the Locomotive Registers; "Sent to Boulogne 24.4.15", and they were both repatriated by the same route via the Richborough Train Ferry on 30 October, 1916. The other ten locomotives sent over the water were all Kirtley T class 0-6-0Ts which worked over at Boulogne, though not all at the same time.

With no equivalent Richborough on the opposite side of the Channel, it was necessary to extend facilities at one of the regular French ports early in 1915 and the SECR was given the task of extending the marshalling yards and dockyard sidings for the War Department's military base at Boulogne where large depots for ammunition, clothing and food supplies had been set up. Work specified included laying extra sidings for a Royal Engineers Park and ammunition yard and

to extend the capacity of the sorting sidings. The two P tanks assisted first with the construction works and then with the ensuing operations. Bradley states that "before departure 27 and 753 were painted unvarnished olive green with large yellow numerals on the tank sides beneath the letters R.O.D. The Company's name and instructions for return to Ashford Works when requiring major overhaul were inscribed in the cab, together with details of the weight, boiler and firebox. After arrival at Boulogne they were renumbered 5027 and 5753". The cause and moment chosen for repatriation was collision damage to the latter which was sent to Ashford Works for attention to its bunker, cab and left-hand side tank, and probably emerged in the wartime grey livery. During this period the SECR locomotives worked entirely in the Boulogne marshalling yards and dockside lines in a similar fashion to their later work at Dover and Folkestone harbours.

With the return of the emigrés the allocations had once again suffered a complete reshuffle. The auto-fitted members were stationed as follows in 1917: 323 and 754 at Margate, 558 at Orpington and 753 at Battersea, the last mentioned being reported at work early in the year on the Dartford-Gravesend Central workings which served four small halts adjacent to the vital Thameside cement and paper mills between Greenhithe and Northfleet with their swollen workmen's traffic. The non-fitted quartet were 27 at Folkestone which, on arrival back from France, had been painted in SECR grey on Dover shed, 178 at Bricklayers Arms, 325 and 555 at Ashford.

Other Governmental Service

Besides those at Richborough, others of the class were commandeered to work Government lines within the SECR system. The reason behind the allocation of 325 and 555 to Ashford in 1917 was to supply motive power for the War Department railway which left the Folkestone main line at Westenhanger (Racecourse Station) to serve both Lympne Camp on the Downs and the aerodrome there. The construction was underway at the end of 1917, with a P tank loaned to the military authorities to help with the work. It was the only SECR class permitted over this goods only branch. Complete by April, 1918, traffic was invoiced to 'Westenhanger for Lympne Camp siding'. Col. J. W. Pringle's inspection in August of the layout of Westenhanger is described by David Gould in 'The SECR in the 1914-18 War.

At the end of 1918 departures from Westenhanger to Lympne were booked at 8.30 and 10.30 a.m. and 1.30 p.m., returning at 9.20 and 11.20 a.m. and 2.20 p.m., the journey taking twenty minutes. If extra trips were needed to fetch empty aeroplane vans from Lympne, special arrangements for such workings were arranged by Ashford Control with the Locomotive Department for relief footplate crews. Bradley mentions that at one stage both locomotives were required daily, one leaving Ashford at 6.50 a.m. and the other at 8.30 a.m. Because of the steep gradients the maximum loadings, inclusive of brake vans, were restricted to ten wagons and the load could not exceed 70 tons down the line and 100 between the Camp and Westenhanger. It was frequently necessary to resort to double heading when the sidings at either end of the line became congested. By February, 1919, the workings were down to two trips each morning, and the traffic continued to fall away with the rapid run down of the Forces.

Another similar enterprise was the 3 ½ mile branch on the Isle of Thanet which ran south-eastwards from the Kent coast line, half a mile west of Birchington, to the R.A.F. camp at Manston Aerodrome. The SECR laid a siding connection with the Up main line between Birchington and Herne Bay stations for the so called Manston Camp Light Railway. The branch line fell for over a mile towards the main line with a

maximum gradient of 1 in 72. There were no significant engineering works, and local roads and tracks were intersected by seven crossings on the level. The maximum speed permitted was 10 mph. Work was completed by 28 July, 1918. The Board of Trade inspection on 22 August referred in detail to the layout as illustrated in David Gould's accompanying diagram, reproduced with his kind permission.

Initially the workings were in the hands of Q class 0-4-4Ts but by 1920 the line was worked by P class members stationed at Margate West, among them at various times 323, 555, 558 and 754, the class being represented there until just before the Grouping. On Mondays to Fridays a goods train left Margate West at 9.10 a.m., Birchington 'A' Junction 9.45-10.05 a.m., arriving at Manston Camp at 10.20 a.m. The train returned at 11.35 a.m., taking fifteen minutes to the junction and was back at Margate at 12.25 p.m. On Saturday the departure was timed for 8.40 a.m. and ran half an hour earlier throughout. It left Manston at 10.25 a.m. for Birchington only, the engine returning light to Manston to work the 11.30 a.m. passenger train to Herne Bay. The two through coaches, which formed the train for R.A.F. personnel and baggage for London, were a bogie Third brake next to the engine and a bogie First saloon. Full details of this and the reverse workings of the locomotives and coaches appear on page 18 of 'The SECR in the 1914-18 War'. By 1925 engines of the A 0-4-4T (LCDR), O and O1 0-6-0s as well as classes P and Q were permitted, but traffic was well in decline. The line itself closed a few years later, and has disappeared almost without a trace. On both these aerodrome lines the traffic mainly consisted of bogie aircraft vans, fuel tankers and flat wagons carrying aero-engines.

In January, 1917, Bricklayers Arms was allocated its first member of the class, receiving 178 from Redhill where it had put in a spell as carriage pilot. 178 was to break new ground, running light early each morning via Lewisham and Blackheath to shunt at the large Royal Flying Corps Aeronautical Stores depot at Kidbrooke, a siding laid by June, 1918, about 220 yards on the London side of Kidbrooke signal cabin. It moved the short distance to Orpington on 1 February, 1919, when the Otford shuttle service was restored.

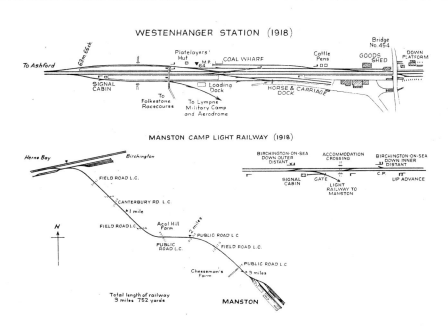

Wartime Passenger Duties

As will be apparent from the preceding paragraphs, the allocation of the P class remained in a constant flux for the duration of the war and, with all these comings and goings, the record of the movements of the class during the war years with their curtain of secrecy is far from complete. There must have been a considerable interchange and moving around to cover members in works or on loan to the Government and to fill in for railcars as they came to be laid aside. The war had brought numerous curtailments and closures on minor routes besides a gradual easing out of the class from duties on which it was obvious that the small boilered tank engines with limited coal capacity were deficient, especially in power ratio. This was very apparent with the sets of three and four carriages worked on the Reading-Ash and Otford-Sevenoaks services.

The writing was already on the wall when Maunsell inaugurated trials in September 1914, which Bradley mentions in some detail: "R 0-4-4T 675 was equipped with motor train gear and, sandwiched between two three-coach sets, ran trials between Moorgate Street and Brixton, Snow Hill and Crystal Palace, and Victoria and Greenwich Park. The P class wire, rod and pulley had not proved entirely satisfactory, especially in cold weather, and therefore compressed air from the Westinghouse pump was used to adjust the engine regulator from the carriage driving compartment." This became standard practice. Brief trials followed on the Gravesend Central-Port Victoria, Dunton Green-Westerham and Paddock Wood-Hawkhurst services. R1 0-4-4T 703 was similarly equipped and worked the Moorgate-Brixton motor train services and some of the Victoria-St Paul's trains. On Sundays both engines shared the Victoria-Crystal Palace (High level) services which caused Battersea's P allocation to be reduced. In April 1916, following withdrawal of the Moorgate-Brixton and other inner London services, 675 and 703 with the two bogie carriage sets were transferred to Reading and Ash ending the P class sequence there.

Also withdrawn as the war progressed were the Beckenham Junction trains to Norwood Junction and to Crystal Palace (low level), Nunhead to Greenwich Park and Otford to Sevenoaks. Although losing their strongest preserves, they briefly took over duties from the diminishing fleet of railcars which included Beckenham Junction -New Beckenham and Elmers End-Hayes.

The Bexhill West Branch

In spite of wartime demands one of the class was commandeered to take over a new passenger duty on unfamiliar territory with the transfer to Hastings of 178 together with a three coach motor train on 1 December 1915, for working the branch to Bexhill where engine and train stabled overnight, visiting Hastings for maintenance and boiler washout. This branch had been authorised by the Crowhurst, Sidley and Bexhill Railway Act of 1897 which was later vested in the South-Eastern, "probably the last competitive line to be opened", according to Dr Edwin Course. It opened on 1 June 1902 from a new spaciously laid out junction at Crowhurst and crossed the impressive Sidley viaduct of nine million bricks on its 4 ½ mile track to Bexhill station, sited just over a mile from the town itself. Bexhill had just become the first resort to allow mixed bathing, but the SEC station relied for patronage on a handful of commuters and local passengers. However by P class standards there had been overcrowding at both ends of the day and in March 1916 178 was replaced by Q1 class 0-4-4T 224 and conventional carriages, and 178 spent the rest of the year as station pilot at Redhill.

The Hastings-Rye Motor Service

Early in 1915 325 had been refitted with auto-train gear and worked a spell between Hastings and Rye, returning again after the Armistice, joined in September 1919 by 323 and later by 754 and took over the Rye services completely with the withdrawal of Railcars 2 and 7 until these duties ceased in September 1921, one frequently acting as Hastings station pilot. The line between Hastings and Rye comprised the sinuous hilly section of the SER Hastings to Ashford route, opened in 1851, which included a ruling gradient of 1 in 90 and started with a climb out of Hastings at 1 in 60. The opening in 1888 of a new station to serve the rapidly expanding residential suburb of Ore (together with carriage sidings in the first open space available beyond Hastings) was a pointer to the future holiday resort development and a salubrious area for retirement. To cater for expanding local traffic the steam railmotors were introduced in 1907 on the section to Rye. Halts were opened at Three Oaks, Guestling (later Doleham) and Snailham, the latter's original wooden platforms of railmotor length surviving till closure in 1959. Two railmotors took over the busy new local service of ten trains a day, two of which went on to Appledore.

As the war drew to a close the traffic along this coastal section exceeded the railmotors' capacity, and 325 was despatched from Ashford, refitted with modified auto-train gear and, always immaculately turned out, worked the service until the end of the 1921 summer timetable. As elsewhere a railmotor remained as a standby till early 1920, the last active role played by the class apart from the later use of their coach portions. Four of them, paired in two articulated sets 513/4 were used on the Sheppey Light Railway auto-trains, the other four as two non-articulated 2-sets 481/2 served on the Isle of Wight from 1925-7, returning to the mainland where they were best known on the Westerham branch.

Before leaving the railmotors, it is worth mentioning those services worked by them on which apparently P tanks do not appear to have been recorded as operating. These include Woodside-Selsdon Road , Deal-Minster, Folkestone-Elham and Lydd-New Romney (the latter on brief trials only.). The proximity of several of the latter to the lines worked by the P class, or sheds where they were stationed must leave the question inconclusively open.

A quiet interlude between services at Rye's eastbound platform before the return to Hastings, as a member of the station staff, the driver and the young fireman, keeping his place at the cab door of No. 754, pose for the photographer.   *Lens of Sutton*

Rye again in 1921 with No. 325 awaiting custom as it stands in the westbound platform ready to return to Hastings. As with so many former SER stations, the platforms were staggered, being linked midway by a foot crossing over the tracks.   *Author's collection*

Changes in Livery and Detail

The wartime period also saw two important changes with regard to their condition. The first concerned the Company's elaborate and expensive livery over which the Directors had made representations without success whilst Harry Wainwright was still in the saddle. In November, 1913, he resigned owing to ill health through overwork. His dozen years of retirement were occupied with local life at Ashford, as a J.P. for the County of Kent and a member of the County Association, and during the War as an officer in the Territorial Army. He died at Bexhill-on-Sea in 1925, aged 60.

R.E.L.Maunsell, who had come from Inchicore to take over, felt that his predecessor's livery was far too good and costly for general use, and within a year the elaborate lining of those engines emerging from the paint shop had been greatly simplified. But the outbreak of the war called for harsher measures, for by 1915 labour and materials were already in short supply. Moreover the Operating Department desired to adopt the American Despatch System of train control, based on the number of the locomotive hauling each train, and requiring the provision of large easily readable numerals. Maunsell therefore used an unlined green with large unshaded yellow figures painted across the tank sides. This livery is shown in the picture of 178 at Bricklayers Arms where the Company's initials appeared astride the number to read "SE 178 CR". This only produced confusion of legibility, and early in 1916 only the number was painted on, supplemented by cast metal rectangular plates lettered "S.E & C.R." attached to the side sheets of the bunker. These plates began to disappear from the 1930's onwards. The 1919 photograph shows 178 carrying sets of Company letters both on the side tank and bunker.

The early wartime livery was still not satisfactory, the yellow numerals becoming illegible through lack of cleaning,

so in 1916 Maunsell introduced his austerity grey livery with a zinc base which turned to black within a few months, and superimposed the large numerals in zinc white. So as the P tanks went to Ashford for a general overhaul, the passenger green livery which had been as recently applied as 1913 to 178, 323, 555 and 754 gave way to the uninspiring grey black which was applied to all the brass work. At the same time a start was made in removing the copper-capped chimneys. According to D.L.Bradley, all this actually pleased the footplate crews who had often complained of being blinded by the sun's reflections on the highly polished brass domes, while the signalmen and staff in general had found considerable difficulty in reading the brass numerals or small number-plates, especially at speed.

Other changes of a mechanical nature were not nearly so obvious. On the instructions of Maunsell, who considered the original working pressure needlessly high for shunting engines, the working pressure was reduced to 160 lb. per sq. in. The dates appear in the Repair Register (Table A) which shows that at the same time opportunity was taken in most cases to renew tubes. There were healthy and unhealthy members of the class, 178 and 754 (the pair at Ash) requiring seven visits each to Ashford up to the Grouping while 555 and 753 got by with three. The largest mileage between repairs was in fact the 74,303 of 754 between January, 1911 and January, 1913. The lowest was an extraordinary 120 of 558 between February, 1918, and July, 1919, which the Repair Register notes as "Ex Richboro". There the scope for shunting on and off the Train Ferry may well have been somewhat confined, but the more likely explanation is a long lay off after mechanical failure which required a General repair at Ashford. 754's large mileage is partly explained by its entering service a good year before most of the rest of the class.

No. 178 in the early wartime livery of unlined olive green with yellow numerals and the Company's initials fitted in either side of the number, together with bunker plates which were fitted later. Taken at Bricklayers Arms where the locomotive was based for the two years from January 1917. *Author's collection*

No. 27 inside Dover Priory locomotive shed wearing the wartime grey livery it received following its repatriation from Boulogne and visit to Ashford Works in the autumn of 1916. *Rail Archive Stephenson*

TABLE A   LOCOMOTIVE REPAIR REGISTER 1910 TO GROUPING 1/23

No.	No. of General Repairs	No. of Light Repairs	Boiler Number	Boiler Pressure Reduced	Second Hand Tubes	Other Replacements	Total Mileages To Date
27	4	1	289	3/19			183,294* 12/23
178	4	3	641	1/17	11/15 1/17	Copper Fire Box 1/17	213,848 9/22
323	4	0	489	11/17	5/15 11/17		195,074 9/23
325	4	2	809	1/17			110,050 4/22
555	3	0	815	4/17	4/17		182,324 6/23
558	4	2	106	2/18	7/14 4/16	Copper Tube Plate 4/16	108,931 11/21
753	3	0	805	11/16	8/13 11/16		103,512*
754	5	2	5	12/17	5/14 12/17	Copper Tube Plate 5/14	308,053 9/23

* Incomplete as mileages, if recorded over at Boulogne, appear to be missing.

At their first general repair in November and February 1911 respectively, 753 and 754 had the lever reversing removed and replaced by the standard Ashford steam system, the cylinders being attached vertically to the front of the right hand side tanks. At the same time, according to Bradley the polished chimney caps and dome covers were painted over and the wheels rebalanced for steadier running at speed. Modifications were also made to the spark arrester and blast pipe to sharpen the blast and clear the rear of the smokebox of deposited ash.

TABLE B   SELECTED P TANK TRAIN SERVICES 1912-22

Route	1912 Normal Weekday	Extra Workings	Sundays	1922 Normal Weekday	Extra Workings	Sundays	Comments
Ash-Aldershot	19	1SO	11	19	1SO	9	
Otford-Sevenoaks	14	4SO	17	11	2SO	None	
Sheppey Light Rly	6	1WSO	4	6	1SO	None	Also 2 empty workings (1922)
Dunton Green - Westerham	15	2SO	8	14	-	8	
Birchington - Ramsgate Sands	4	1ThSO	None	4	1 School Children's 8.5 am from Birchington	None	1st train started from Margate West
Sandgate - Sandling Junction	19	2SO	14	12	2SO	None	2 through Steam Railcars to Dover or Folkestone
Hastings - Rye	6	-	None	5	-	None	1922 3rd Class only

From Grouping to Nationalisation

Seaborne Again

One might have imagined that with the close of the War the sea-travels of the class would be at an end, but the Southern Railway came into being with something of a crisis involving the Isle of Sheppey, with the Ashford Engine Repair books recording for locomotives 325 (ex-Hastings) and 558 (ex-Margate West) on 3 January, 1923: "To be prepared and sent to Sheppey. Not to be counted as a repair."

The emergency arose like this. The 1904 built Kings Ferry lifting bridge across the River Swale which separated Sheppey from the mainland seemed to have, in R.W.Kidner's words, "a fatal fascination for absent-minded helmsmen." On 17 December, 1922, the Canadian SS Gyp bound for Ridham Dock struck the said bridge leaving the island isolated and this resulted in the closure of the railway for ten months. As from 27 December Sheerness passengers were catered for by a service to Port Victoria and a steamer across the water, but Leysdown passengers were still without transport. A Peckett 0-6-0ST was borrowed from Settle Speakman's coal wharf at Queenborough to provide a token service. Meanwhile orders had gone out to call two P tanks to Ashford, 325 arriving on 28 December, and 558 two days later, and the locomotives given a quick inspection over the New Year period. They left auto-fitted on 3 January, 1923, for Slades Green Depot where they were taken apart, put into wagons and shipped to Sheerness. There they were reassembled and placed on the Leysdown Line, as well as turns on the Sheppey Light Railway and worked a shuttle service from 1 March as far as a temporary platform on the Queenborough side of the Swale bridge until the latter had been repaired, then returning to their former duties, after normal train services resumed on 1 November.

This is the only known photograph taken in 1923 of the temporary platform at Swale Bridge, and of a P class on this shortlived emergency service.

Courtesy Southern Railway Magazine

Photographed from the platform of the Pier station at Folkestone on 24 September 1923, No. 555 on shunting duties forms a backcloth to the network of tracks beside the harbour. *Pamlin Prints*

Southern Railway Changes

The allocations of the remainder at the Grouping were 27, 555, and 754 at Folkestone, 753 at Ashford and auto-fitted 178 and 323 at Tonbridge for the Otford service where motor trains had recommenced running on 1 February 1918 with 178. The quaint coaching stock used for this service in the early 'twenties was a three-coach set of ex-L.C.D.R. six-wheeled vehicles comprising a three compartment brake second (later third), a four compartment first with one given over to third class, and a five compartment third. The latter is mentioned by David Gould in his "Westerham Valley Railway" as having "only half height divisions between the compartments, and there was a spittoon, comprising a hunk of cloth screwed to the floor, at each corner of the compartments", but there is some doubt whether this relic from a less hygienic era was being used at this late date. The SR numbers of the three-coach sets used in the West Kent area and interchangeable as regards the Dartford-Gillingham, Gravesend West Street and the Otford and Westerham services were 649-51, 653 and 677. Between the coaches was a strong bar coupling, but the normal screw coupling was employed at the auto-ends of the set. The ex LCDR bogie sets on the Ash-Aldershot workings were numbered to 732/3.

The effects of the new regime were first made apparent by the transformation of 178 and 325 to the Southern Railway's dark green livery together with their numbers prefixed by an Ashford 'A'. They left the Works together on the afternoon of 22 July, 1924, and gradually the rest assumed this new livery as they passed through Ashford. 753 was transferred to Redhill in the spring of 1923 to act as station pilot. On the last day of 1925 its number was changed to 556 to make way for the numerical sequence of the new L1 class 4-4-0s, the renumbering being carried out at the running shed in large S.E.C. pattern white numerals on the tank sides (it received its 'A' prefix the following November). 754 had been altered earlier on 4 December, 1925, to 557, but had already assumed the new green livery. 325 with the demise of its push-pull duties between Hastings and Rye was sent to Dover in the spring of 1925, and the following year a similar transfer of 323, as heavier loads of increasing commuter traffic ousted the P class from the kind of service for which they had been primarily designed. For the time being they were phased out as a passenger locomotive, and by the autumn of 1926 all push-pull gear had been removed permanently from the class.

No. 178 in charge of the Otford shuttle whiles away time in the back siding at Sevenoaks until its next turn of duty. In 1922 the coaches still offered all three classes of travel.

H.J.P. Rutherford Collection/NRM York

Renumbering was necessitated by making clear a numerical sequence for the new L1 class 4-4-0s. No. 753 is seen shunting at Redhill on 30 May 1925. By good fortune it and its companion No. 754 were able to be fitted in to a P class sequence between 555 and 558.

LCGB Ken Nunn Collection

The 'new' No. 556 is at the platform at Redhill coupled to an interesting GWR clerestory coach which has arrived on one of the through workings from Reading on May Day 1926.

H.C.Casserley

3 April 1926, the final year of P class workings on the Otford shuttle. No. 323 stands between the platforms at Sevenoaks in the sedate era prior to electrification.

H.C.Casserley

No. A558 was the member of the class sent to the West Country for tests on the Wenford Bridge and Lyme Regis branches. Fortunately for the sake of our future heritage the trials were unsuccessful, or the ancient Beattie well tanks and the Adams radial tanks might not have survived to be preserved in the early 1960s.

Real Photographs

Numbered A556 and now in Southern livery, this locomotive had by May 1927 moved up to Battersea, based there for employment in the construction of the Wimbledon and Sutton Railway.

F.R.Hebron/Rail Archive Stephenson

In the West

1928 was a red letter year for the class as they broke new ground, not just on the Western Section but at its furthest extremities with the arrival of A558 in the summer of 1928 at Wadebridge for trials on the Wenford Bridge china clay line where it was hoped the aged Beattie well tanks might be replaced. But the six-coupled wheels took unkindly to the many sharp curves, and the P failed to give satisfaction. For the same reason a week's trial on the Lyme Regis branch produced no fruitful results and the Adams radial tanks remained ensconced there for another thirty years and more. A558 was noted passing Halwill Junction en route from Wadebridge.

Trio of Contractors Locomotives

A558 returned in the early autumn of 1928 from its adventures in far West to the near West. It joined A556 which had been at Battersea (ex - L.B.S.C.) shed since its Redhill spell, and A555 which came up specially from Dover, to assist with the new works of the Wimbledon and Sutton Railway. Though a vital new commuter suburban link line, in terms of the era of railway construction this was very much an afterthought. The SR initially decided to undertake the construction itself and, needing small wheeled lightweight tank locomotives, it found suitable substitutes within its own ranks in the P class tanks.

In the "Southern Railway Magazine" for October, 1928, "Astodos", the incognito scribe for the London West notes, reported: "Work on the Wimbledon and Sutton Railway progresses apace. There is the jolliest little Eastern Section tank engine engaged on construction at the Wimbledon end, and such is the admiration bestowed upon it that I am afraid someone will steal it one night and take it home as a pet!" The January, 1930 issue of the magazine reported the line completed

and showed a picture of the construction at St. Helier in which a P tank can be distantly discerned standing in the platform. The SR in fact after building one mile at the Wimbledon end, left Sir Robert McAlpine & Co. to carry on to Sutton using standard and narrow gauge Hudswell Clark tank engines.

Renumbering

In 1931 the Southern Railway introduced its new renumbering scheme. 1000 was added to the numbers of Eastern Section engines and the 'A' omitted, and from 1936, since they were now classified as humble goods shunting engines, the P class were to be repainted in unlined goods black livery. These changes were implemented as the class visited Ashford, but A558, always a lingerer, managed to evade the issue, retaining its early Southern number and green livery until January, 1940, by which time a further change of style had taken place and the numerals were painted on the bunker sides instead of on the side tanks. However in 1938 the copper cap chimneys and brass bands of 1557 and A558 were still proudly polished.

Decline in Mileage

With transfer from passenger workings after the Grouping to light shunting duties, annual mileages dropped sharply from the 20,000 to 30,000 range to around 10,000. The best annual figures were early in the SR era, notably 323's 14,433 miles/year at its overhaul in January 1927, and 557's annual average of 14,219 up to July 1927; the worst performers were 325 and 555 with figures regularly around 7000 per year. But, according to Peter Cooper, for most of the post grouping period these figures avoid the question - how does one accurately measure and record the mileage run by a shunting engine?

This interesting rear side view of No. 1027 renumbered at Ashford Works shows the mid-period Southern unlined black livery to advantage, including the additional numerals at the back of the coal bunker. The date is 25 April 1936.

H.C.Casserley

Folkestone

The 'thirties were for the class the most settled years of its existence. Under the S.E & C.R. the small shed at Folkestone Junction, providing cover for six tank engines, had its own separate coding, but under the Southern it became a sub-shed to the new main depot at Dover Marine opened in 1928. Though nominally all Folkestone engines were allocated to Dover, the Southern continued to state specifically which were at Dover and which were at the sub-depot; the latter retained a large measure of independence through to the 1940s. In 1933, for instance, Dover had 1323, 1555 and 1557, Ashford A558, and Folkestone the rest.

The Folkestone engines were used on light shunting duties on the short wheelbase sidings at the Harbour end. The shunting there before the P tanks arrived was in the hands of two ancient veterans. The earlier of these to be posted there was 752 in March, 1904, an 0-6-0ST constructed in September, 1879, by Manning Wardle & Co. It acquired the name *Grinstead* when new in Joseph Firbank's ownership during the construction of the Lewes-East Grinstead Railway between 1879 and 1881. It was purchased by William Rigby in 1899 and used on various contracts including the Folkestone Pier Extension, and on completion in 1904 was bought by the S.E & C.R. in order to continue to work its newly constructed territory. Locally it was known as "Thumper" because of the noise it made at any speed above ten miles per hour, which it achieved when running down the steep grade to the quays from the shed at Folkestone Junction. It lasted there until August, 1925, when it was decided that further repairs were not justified in view of the P tanks then becoming available for the light harbour work.

Its companion was old "Little Tich", the Terrier 751, fitted with a specially constructed Wainwright boiler between 1910 and 1932, and posted to Folkestone in mid-1916 following a brief filling in turn for a P at Richborough. It was sent to Battersea on being replaced by the first P tank to arrive in mid-1919. This was 27, joined in the autumn by 754 and the following year for a brief spell by 178, returning there again following the end of its duties on the Otford service. In 1923, 555 arrived from Margate but was posted to Dover to be joined by 27, but after the Wimbledon-Sutton duty in 1928/9 was back at Folkestone with 178, 323, 325, and 557. So it was that between 1934 and 1938 all eight engines were close together for the first time in their lives, allocated to "Dover cum-Folkestone." In 1937 Dover had 1027, 1178 and 1323, Folkestone had the rest.

Dover Harbour

The story of the development of the harbour area into the busiest passenger port in Britain is a complex one originating out of the S.E. and the L.C.D.'s Victorian rivalry. The need for further expansion resulted in the completion of the 'Admiralty Harbour' in 1909, the replacement of the original Dover Pier by the Marine Station effected at the end of 1914 in time for the vast upsurge in military traffic and the modernised continental services in 1919, the rationalisation of surplus lines and stations in the area, and the considerable reclamation behind the sea wall of land on which a new locomotive depot was opened in 1928 replacing the old one at Dover Priory.

Adjacent to the Marine Station which was built on reclaimed land inside the Admiralty Pier was the train ferry dock, designated the New Channel Ferry Pier, and then sweeping around the Harbour from the South Pier came Clarence Quay, Custom House Quay, Granville Dock and North Pier, behind which was Union Street. It was along this road that the dockside lines entered this part of the harbour, connected to the ex-L.C.D.R. main line by a trailing junction in the short gap between the harbour tunnel and station. The lines continued up the length of Prince of Wales Quay and Pier, opened in 1900-2. In 1907 a coal and petroleum depot was opened on the eastern arm and, to serve a further section of the docks, the lines were extended across a new bridge over the entrance to Wellington docks to serve Commercial Quay, and along the promenade and Waterloo Crescent to provide a rail link for the growing number of factories built in the Eastern Docks.

It was this complex of sharp curved tramway type harbour lines for which the P tanks were ideally suited and they served right through to their final demise. Starting with a brief visit by 555 in 1912, following the Grouping all the class sooner or later gravitated there, based first at Dover Priory shed and then at the new Marine shed. There was full work for about three with one or two usually in store in the quiet season, and members seem to have come in for more photography inside the back of Dover shed than out on the less accessible harbour lines. One was regularly employed on the Channel Ferry duties, while another worked the street tramway and the eastern promenade, being the only engines prior to the 1939-45 war to work along the sea front at Dover. Another was used occasionally as pilot at the Priory (Town) station in the earlier period, and on occasions a member of the class may have been made available to help at one of the nearby Kent coalfield collieries. Indeed it appears that a member of the class was loaned to the Horton Institute of the London County Council in 1936, repeated again in June 1938 when the locomotive in question was 1555.

The busy quayside at Folkestone on 14 May 1927 as the SS Biarritz unloads its passengers. No. A27 waits with its flat wagons for the crane to lower registered containers off the ship. A fine harbour scene of yesteryear. *H.C.Casserley*

A few months later No. A27 was transferred to Dover where it stayed for the majority of its remaining years, being very much a 'Dover engine'. While the engine crew take a nap, the shunters pass away the languorous time of day chatting. *J.E.Simpson*

Another less fortunate pairing were Nos. A558 and A557 seen in the evening light outside Folkestone Junction shed c1930.
Author's collection

A brief moment of fame for the crew of No. A555 at Dover. We have the fireman's name, Bill Ford. This was one of F.Moore's Railway Photographs published from 3 Amen Corner EC4.
Author's collection

Nos. A27 and A323 stand at the back of Dover Priory shed in 1929, a premonition of the time when they would come together again on the Bluebell Railway.
J.A.G.Coltas

Dover in June 1937 as No. 1323 pauses for a family snap by Wellington Dock. The young girl in the wide-brimmed sun hat is the photographer's daughter, Barbara.
F.M.Gates

Kingston Wharf

The Dover monopoly was eventually broken in early April, 1938, when 1323 was firmly allocated to Brighton for shunting the coal stage at the Locomotive depot, and was joined on the 17th by 1557 which commenced service at Kingston Wharf, Shoreham. This had been the Brighton Railway's intended gateway to the Continent and was the initial line to open in 1840. After a few years in use the passenger boat service to Dieppe was shut down as the L.B. & S.C.R. favoured Newhaven, but the goods traffic via the wharf sidings continued in use. These were connected with the station buildings by a cable-worked incline at right angles to the lines at each end, and each wagon had to be turned on the table. The haulage up the incline was by a steam winding engine which took steam from a spare locomotive stationed behind it. Shunting along the wharf was undertaken by horses. Early in 1938 the line was relaid with strengthened track as a through line on a gradient of 1 in 82. It had sharp curves and a small engine was required and, needless to say, the P class was called in though 756 *A.S. Harris*, the ex-P.D.S.W.J. engine was given a short trial there. This turn became a P preserve until almost the end, apart from the opening months of the Second War when B4s 91 and 92 replaced them. 1323 returned to Brighton in February, 1940, and 1557 two months later. Terriers were not allowed to work on Kingston Wharf owing to buffer interlocking.

Kingston Wharf, Shoreham, in 1938, the last year when shunting was carried out by horses, after which members of the P class based at Brighton took over the duties. *H.M.Madgwick*

The new regime at Kingston Wharf on 4 May 1938 in the shape of No. 1323. *H.M.Madgwick*

On Loan to the KESR

The post-Grouping gravitation of the class at Channel coast ports was briefly interrupted at intervals when several were loaned on hire to the independent Kent and East Sussex Railway. At this stage of its history that private concern had but a mere handful of serviceable locomotives; the rest of the stock lay in Rolvenden yard in varying degrees of disintegration, and there was little likelihood of there being finance to ever get these back into service for they had been steadily eroded by cannibalisation for spare parts. Those not already written off in 1937/8 lingered on awhile until contributing to the wartime scrap metal effort, being officially broken up in 1941. It only needed one of the viable locomotives to go away for a major overhaul to create a motive power crisis.

So far there has been no confirmation of a report in a *Railway Magazine* article stating that on 20 August 1931 a Robertsbridge - Headcorn mixed train was hauled by a P class 0-6-0T, whether on trial for possible purchase or to cover an acute shortage of stock. Unfortunately W.H.Austen's register, held by today's Tenterden Railway Company, of Steam Train Mileages only commences in August 1932. These cover the period to May 1948 during which the KESR had to rely heavily on locomotives hired or lent by the Southern Railway, having from 1938 through to 1947 anything from three to six locomotives on hire in the course of a year.

First of a long line in November 1936 was 1556, brought in while Terrier No. 3 *Bodiam* was away at Ashford. It stayed two months, the pioneer of a succession of Terriers, ex-LSWR 0330s and 0395s, ex-SECR 01s and further P class engines. 1556 returned for a further nine month spell in 1938. There was then a gap until 1325 arrived in July 1945. It has been suggested that, though well suited to the light peacetime traffic, they were not considered sturdy enough for the heavier wartime loads.

The KESR made the best possible use of the P Class locomotives hired out to them. With their ten ton axle load, the class were admirably suited to the section between Tenterden and Robertsbridge but there is ample photographic evidence available that they were equally acceptable on the northern Headcorn section. The P class members were in use nearly every working day during their periods on the line. 1325 had been loaned to Rolvenden while Terrier 2678 was away in Ashford Works at a period when traffic was quite brisk compared with the pre-war days. It stayed until the following September before returning to Dover. In March 1947, 1555 arrived while Terrier No. 3 was absent in Brighton Works for a heavy overhaul. It served through to September when it was decided to hire 1556 instead for the final fortnight of that month when KESR No. 3 returned from Brighton. Nationalisation at the close of the year put a completely different complexion on motive power availability on the absorbed KESR.

No. 1556, on loan to the independent Kent & East Sussex Railway, heads a train approaching Tenterden St. Michael's on Easter Monday 1938.   *Stewart Dewsbery*

Whistling furiously approaching the ungated crossing, No. 1325 brings in the 11.15 am, comprising a second hand LSWR coach from Rolvenden into Tenterden Town on 7 September 1946. The elaborate but inoperative signal was typical of this run down line.   *LCGB Ken Nunn Collection*

The 4.20 pm Tenterden Town to Robertsbridge is seen leaving Tenterden behind No. 1555 on 23 August 1947. Nationalisation the following year brought loans of members of the class to an end as Terriers were drafted in and held sway till the line's closure.   *S.C.Nash*

World War II

The war had hardly begun when on 6 September 1939, following a chalk fall in Folkestone Warren, the Folkestone-Dover main line was closed temporarily to all traffic. The request came for a P class locomotive to run light from Folkestone to Dover, diverted via the Elham Valley line and Canterbury. But crossing staff were unprepared for special traffic at short notice and the P tank in question crashed through Duck Street Crossing gates at Elham. Damage to the locomotive was minimal and it proceeded on to Canterbury West. There it was learned that it was not needed at Dover after all, and ordered to return to Folkestone, back down the Elham Valley line.

At the outbreak of the Second World War 1323 and 1557 were at Brighton, 1178 and 1325 at Dover and the remainder outshedded at Folkestone. In November 1939, the class were passed for running ambulance trains for wartime casualties on the Hellingly Hospital railway, but it is doubtful if they were ever used, following a decision to use Netley Hospital instead for this traffic. A member of the class was noted attending to a derailment on the Bedenham Sidings branch in the area around that time. In the first half of 1940, 1178 and 1325 were transferred to Folkestone, and 1556 and 1558 to Gillingham as part of the evacuation of coastal sheds because of likely air raids or cross Channel bombardment. The Gillingham pair, though officially in store, appear to have been pressed into service by the demands of the occasion, assisting with the banking of troop trains consisting of LMS or LNER coaches headed out of Chatham Dockyard by an F1 or B1. An observer described the pair of P tanks as "puffing frantically in the rear".

Brave 1027 was left alone at Dover, which established its reputation as a "Dover Engine" and became a firm favourite with the locomen there to the very end of its days. In September, 1943, 1323 was on loan to Snowdown Colliery just up the line at Canterbury, while 1178 filled in at Brighton. At the end of the War the allocation stood at 1178 and 1557 at Brighton, 1323 and 1558 at Folkestone and the other four at Dover.

The Final Years of the Southern

The situation continued as ever to be complicated by the constant shifting around as members of the class went through the various works, and the general run down of major maintenance during the war years caused a close succession of works visits during the last period of the Southern Railway; 1556 Ashford summer 1945; 1027 Ashford October 1945; 1557 Ashford early 1946; 1178 Ashford summer 1946; 1323 Ashford December, 1946; 1558 Ashford spring, 1947; 1178 Stewarts Lane April, 1947; 1557 Brighton December, 1947; 1178 Brighton January, 1948; 1555 Ashford April, 1948; 1325 Ashford December, 1948.

When 1557 visited Ashford, Dover's 1555 went over to Brighton as replacement, taking over the coal stage shunt. Brighton Ps travelling to or from Ashford frequently made an overnight stop at Eastbourne shed. Although two P tanks were shedded at Brighton, they rarely exchanged duties, 1178 being used consistently at Kingston Wharf. When the latter visited Ashford, B4 dock tank 88 had a turn at Shoreham, but when 1178 found its way back to a former haunt at Bricklayers Arms for light overhaul early in 1947, P tanks were again in such short supply that B4s 83 and 89 covered the Brighton duties. Ashford was so overwhelmed by the backlog of repairs that some of the class had to be farmed out elsewhere, and in the last month of the old regime 1557 entered the sanctum of Brighton Works, while occasionally members were later sent to Longhedge repair shop which lay at the back of Stewarts Lane depot.

Apart from Brighton which hosted 1178 and 1557 at Nationalisation, the hardest work was still done at Dover which had allocated, 1027, 1325, 1555 and 1556. Some mighty work must have been in store for the last mentioned in the early summer of 1946 as it filled in with 01 0-6-0s and E2 0-6-0Ts on the train ferry turn removing surplus WD 2-8-0s minus coupling rods and motion, returning from France off the train ferry steamers. To quote the *Railway Observer* for July 1946: 'A small SR 0-6-0T, generally 1556, can often be seen removing these engines from the ferry.' It was Dover depot that was always called upon whenever there was a shortage on the KESR. 1323 and 1558 lingered at Folkestone with lengthy periods in store, 1558 inordinately so judging by the chalked inscriptions which seemed to imply that the old warrior was ripe for scrapping. But the new powers that be proclaimed otherwise.

Nationalisation and its Aftermath

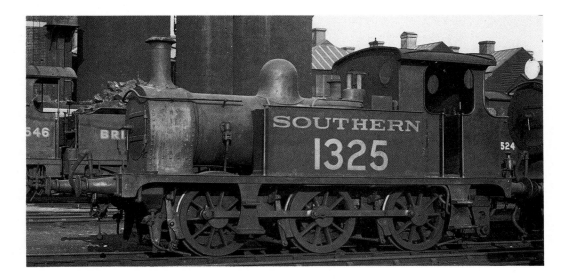

British Railways initial livery is evident on Brighton shed on 14 August 1948 on two members of the ex-LBSC C2X class, but No. 1325 has survived to Nationalisation in the pre-war Southern lettering and livery.

J.H.Aston

Western Section Assignments

The opening year of the new regime saw little of event apart from the odd shed transfer and the gradual introduction of the early British Railways liveries. The class was classified 0F until 1953, after which it was considered "unclassified". But in 1949 things began to move in spectacular fashion. July witnessed the arrival of 31325 at Eastleigh shed where it had been sent for use at Winchester because withdrawal was causing a shortage of B4 dock tanks which had made the shunting duties at the station goods yard their particular niche. There was an extensive and important yard there reached by a sharp curve which could only be negotiated by a short wheelbase locomotive. From L.S.W. days a shunter had been outstationed from Eastleigh, a coal stage being constructed for its use in 1920 and a small shed provided in 1928. A railway correspondent wrote: "There cannot be many places left in the country where an individual station has its own shunting engine allocated with its own small shed - subshed to Eastleigh."

And if that was not enough 31325 actually reached as far west as the running shed at Bournemouth Central which was

also feeling the temporary shortage of B4s, the regulars on the Poole Harbour-Hamworthy goods branch, the allocation for which was two of the class. It was kept at Bournemouth as a spare while B4 30087 was repaired by Eastleigh Works, but does not appear to have been used and was put in store when the B4 returned in August. Next month it was taken out and returned to Eastleigh for some light repairs before resuming the Winchester goods shunt. In mid-November it broke more new ground by working the once daily pick-up goods on the Bishops Waltham branch on a day when the regular M7 tank 242 had a boiler washout. It remained a regular employee in the yard shunting at Winchester City until January, 1951, when it was replaced by B4 30102, and returned via Fratton to Brighton. Before this happened a second P had appeared at Eastleigh in April, 1950, in the shape of 1558, still in S.R. livery, which was reported to have been on loan to the R.N. Armaments Depot at Bedenham. It was little if at all used after this and before its transfer to Stewarts Lane. It returned yet again to Eastleigh for a further spell in the summer of 1953.

No. 31325 with a blank tankside as it stands outside Eastleigh MPD in 1949 in the company of ex-LBSC E1 class 0-6-0T No. s2133.
Author's collection

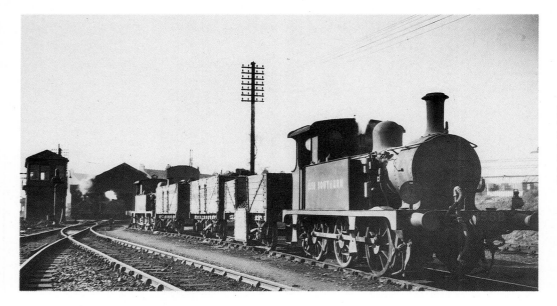

The sun sets on Folkestone Junction shed and on its P class allocation. No. 1558 ekes out its time on coaling duties while fellow member No. 1555 sits out of steam against the buffers. 19 February 1949. *D.Trevor Rowe*

Later in the same year No. 1558, still proudly bearing its wartime Southern livery, languishes out of steam and out of water with chalked indications that its water tanks have been empty since the beginning of the month. *S.C.Nash*

Trials at Dover

In the late autumn of 1949, soon after the chalk besmirched photograph of 1558 had been taken at Folkestone, it came out of store to help Dover's 31027 and 1557 (which had exchanged its Brighton allocation with 31556 in May) on the sea front promenade haulage to the Eastern Docks, traffic for which had increased steadily following the expansion of an oil depot there and preparations for a new car ferry terminal which was opened in 1953. Furthermore at this period parts of locomotives scrapped at Ashford were carried to the yard of Dover Industries Ltd, a scrap metal firm sited adjacent to the eastern arm of the harbour; track to this yard was relaid and set in concrete. The train was always preceded on this stretch of almost a mile in length by a man with a red flag whose job included the rounding up of cars parked across the lines with willing assistance from bystanders. The sight never failed to provide an amusing diversion for holiday makers, but this was added to by the fact that the increasing loads stretched to the limit the power of the diminutive P tanks who were expected to pull anything up to 20 loaded wagons along the promenade.

A spectator described the antics as follows: "Two thirds of the way along the Sea Front the procession stops, and the steep curve onto the Prince of Wales Pier is charged at speed with about 9 wagons. Even with 8 loaded wagons a few weeks ago 31557 made two unsuccessful charges before succeeding on the third attempt. Some interested spectators cheered!" But the M.P.D. authorities were obviously concerned at the increasing loads and eventually on 14 October, 1951, trials were carried out along the sea front to the Eastern Docks between 31178 and B4 30084. The P managed 20 wagons and the B4 was successful with 28. As a result a decree went forth that Dover Sea Front haulage was to be in the hands of a B4, relieved when necessary by a P.

The busy harbour scene beside Granville Dock at Dover where, in a setting of ships, cranes and warehouses No. 31557 shunts coal wagons. Next to the locomotive is one of the long eight wheel SR Goods brake vans, No. 55663.
P.Ransome Wallis

In august company at Dover No. 31178, nearing its half century span and relegated to looking after the tool vans, takes a sideways glance at 'Britannia' No. 70004 *William Shakespeare* ready to move off shed to take the 'Golden Arrow' express back to London.
Author's collection

No. 31325 stands by the coaling and watering stage at Kingston Wharf in 1950. The snap was given by the ex-driver seen on the footplate.
Courtesy Arthur Bissell

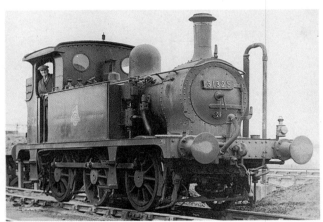

Changes in Allocation

Over at neighbouring Folkestone a representative continued to be employed on light shunting duties down at the harbour. 1555 had been transferred there at the start of 1949 to join 31323 which in November had exchanged places with 1558, the latter quickly returning to Dover. September, 1950, saw the actual end of the Ps at Folkestone (though 31558 was given a theoretical posting there in January, 1959 while in fact at Stewarts Lane). 31555, following a spell at Stewarts Lane from July, 1949, to September, 1950, went back to Dover, and 1558 went to Stewarts Lane instead. At the outset of 1950 31325's move to Brighton had released s1178 to Dover where it later participated in the previously mentioned trial. In the twelve months commencing November, 1951, Dover parted with its three regulars, 31557 which left for Stewarts Lane, as did 31555 exactly a year later, while in between from February

to October, 1952, 31027 went over to Eastleigh where it was photographed with part of the Southern 1027 clearly visible through the later coats of black paint. On the outward journey it had been impounded in store at Fratton during the early spring while its return was notable for a pause at Brighton shed on 5 October, 1952, when three of the class, 31027, 31325 and 31556, were unusually seen there together by railway enthusiasts attending the Brighton Works Centenary. 31027 had reached Eastbourne by mid-November on its way to Ashford for a major shopping, before resuming at Dover.

By 1953 the class had once more settled down, though not for long, at three familiar centres:- 31027, 31178 and 31323 (the latter having just returned from a major overhaul at Ashford) at Dover (74C), 31325 and 31556 at Brighton (75A) and 31555, 31557 and 31558 at Stewarts Lane, Battersea (73A).

No. 31027 was a fast mover in the third quarter of 1952 as recorded separately by three different photographers.

30 August saw it at Eastleigh sandwiched between 02 class No. 30225 and an unrebuilt West Country Pacific. Faded versions of its Southern and early British Railways liveries compete on its tank side.

R.A.Panting

5 October found No. 31027 interrupting its eastward journey at Brighton where a thoughtful railwayman had chalked the correct number on the cab side. *A.R.Goult*

16 November and it stands beside the old shed at Eastbourne displaying its less faded side. It was on its way for repair at Ashford Works before returning to its native Dover. *S.C.Nash*

A view of the inner Western dock area at Dover in the late 1950s at a time of still relative prosperity. At least three locomotives can be seen in this aerial photograph, including a P tank near the Strood Street gates where the dockland railway network joined the BR London-Dover main line. It ran alongside the Granville and Wellington Docks, past the coal wharfs of Union Street, and across the Wellington Swing Bridge to the old Prince of Wales Pier then along the seafront to the Eastern Docks.

Photo courtesy Dover Harbour Board

Further Drama at Dover

Dover rarely dropped below its quota of three P tanks for its numerous duties, shunting the Town Yard, the Ferry Dock, the Harbour Board lines and the Eastern Docks, plus filling in with shed pilot and coaling stage duties. Even so the depot found it possible to allocate a member of the class to shunt at one of the various collieries of the Kent coalfield. 1323 had spent the September of 1943 assisting the war effort at Snowdown Colliery, and ten years later was noted there again on loan to the National Coal Board at the end of August, 1953. 31557 had been on loan to Betteshanger Colliery in the summer of 1950, and 31027 was there the following year, while 31178 was at Chislet Colliery during 1955 and 31027 in 1958. Indeed if full records were available it would show that most of the Dover allocated members of the class were working in the coalfields from time to time out of sight to all but the most determined photographers.

31027 also found cause to be absent from base in mid-October, 1955, being despatched to St. Leonards to act as standby engine for the Tenterden goods working at a time when Terriers were in short supply. Apart from Class A1X, the P tanks were the only other steam locomotives permitted to work over the light K.E.S.R. track between Robertsbridge and Tenterden. If 31027 did obtain an opportunity to work this duty, it would have been the first occasion since 1947, for members of the class had ably proved themselves on the K.E.S.R. in the decade prior to nationalisation.

This was but one instance of the increasing interchangeability between the three classes of diminutive, yet dissimilar tank engines used for working light railways and sharp radius sidings, the Southern having inherited one class from each of its pre-grouping constituents. The P tank overlapped the LSW B4s as shunters and the Brighton Terriers on branch duties. The classic instance of such cooperation occurred in that much to be relished incident when ex-L.S.W.R. dock tank 30084 was caught in a violent snowstorm in Dover's Eastern Dock on 10 February, 1956, and had to be abandoned! This was the regular engine, failing which a P tank was to act as relief stand-by. 31027 was therefore sent as replacement to fetch in the wagons, but found the going quite impossible, and its return journey on its own fraught with the greatest difficulty lest it too suffer the B4's fate. One who witnessed the incredible sight described 31027 as "charging about 20 yards at a time, and slipping to a stand, while eight men with shovels tried to clear the track." The unfortunate B4 was eventually rescued by ex-L.B.S.C. Terrier 32670, stationed at Dover at this period.

Emergency Calls

It was the addition of these versatile "foreigners" to Dover's quota that enabled 31178 to wander off on some rare adventures. Proudly bearing its newly acquired 0F classification, it was sent in July, 1953, on loan to Bowater Lloyds Pulp and Paper Mills Ltd., to serve in their standard gauge exchange sidings with B.R. at Ridham Dock in place of their privately owned 0-4-0ST *Jubilee* which was under repair. The latter returned to service in September, but 31178 continued to soldier on till the early autumn.

Another emergency call came towards the close of 1955 when the Stores Siding on the Deptford Wharf branch, for so long the preserve of the ex-L.B.S.C. E6 class, was prohibited to these heavy 0-6-2Ts. 31178, which had been on loan to Chislet Colliery, was moved to Bricklayers Arms in case any movements were required over this line. It is not known whether the P tank actually shunted in the Stores Siding, for following authorisation for diesels to work the Stores line, 31178 was sent away on 11 January, 1956, for a further spell on loan at Ridham Dock. There early in March, 1956, it became a total failure, and on 12 March Dover sent its Terrier 32670 on loan as a replacement. However, things must have been fixed up smartly for 31178 was reported standing in for another member of the class at Brighton on 23 April, but further mechanical difficulties called for a visit to Ashford that November. The September following, 31178 was transferred to Stewarts Lane to replace 31557 withdrawn that month, and on its own withdrawal in June, 1958, it was immediately sold into the familiar hands of Messrs Bowaters for an active retirement, and joined old *Jubilee* on well-trodden duties in the exchange sidings at Ridham Dock.

Above: A rare visitor to Gillingham shed is P class No. 31555, taken shortly before scrapping in 1954. It may have been en route to Bowaters who hired small 0-6-0Ts on occasions before they bought No. 31178.
N. Newman

Left: Dover shed frequently seconded members of its P class allocation to duties in the Kent coalfields. No. 31027 is seen at work at Chislet Colliery on 19 June 1958.
H.C.Casserley

Stewarts Lane

Up at Stewarts Lane, unlike the tight situation at Dover, the allocation of, on occasions, three members of the class was distinctly generous taking into account the limited duties involved, namely coaling stage, shunting the sharply curved milk siding which lay between the carriage sheds and the rear of the Longhedge Works complex, and as occasion demanded helping out with carriage shunting. Following its time on loan to the K.E.S.R., 1555 had gone through Ashford Works in April, 1948, an early recipient of the post-nationalisation livery with "British Railways" across its side tanks, and was then posted the following year to Stewarts Lane. Then in October, 1949, it was decreed that "P tanks may now work into and out of Stewarts Lane Milk Depot as required." In 1950 31555 was exchanged with Dover's 1558, only to return to Stewarts Lane in 1952, to find that 31557 had also been posted there in the intervening year. The sudden influx of P tanks was due to the withdrawal of the longserving ex-L.C.D.R. T class 0-6-0Ts which had been responsible for the coaling stage duties in the post-war years. 1604 went in 1950, and 1602, the last survivor left in July, 1951.

1558 made a special mark for itself by being the last Southern Engine to be renumbered by British Railways, this occurring on 25 July, 1953, following its transfer to Eastleigh, where after some active service at Winchester, it entered a strange period in limbo. The mid-1950s was a time when the Southern Region was particularly keen on recording official lists of its locomotives in store, winter being the chief period when many locomotives were inactive, apart from some taken out temporarily for the seasonal Christmas parcels traffic. Some unfortunates were in store for long periods on end and 31558 was one of these, and this may account for the lack of photographs of this engine in the later B.R. period. At the beginning of 1954 it was in store at Eastleigh, being transferred "while in store!" to Brighton that April. Still in store in May, 1955, it was transferred yet again back full circle to Stewarts Lane where it remained in store until July when it re-entered service.

Its re-emergence was a necessity, for despite occasional turns by visiting B4 dock engines to work the milk siding, the ranks of the Stewarts Line P allocation were growing thin for all the first withdrawals of the class took place from this depot. In January, 1955, 31555 paid a final visit to Ashford Works, but following removal of boiler and tanks the decision was taken to condemn, and it was officially withdrawn the following month. The next to go was 31557, withdrawn in September, 1957, from Stewarts Lane, where it was replaced by the transfer of 31178 which was in turn sold out of service to Messrs Bowaters in June, 1958. By this time the small Drewry diesels were permitted on the milk siding, and 31558 after seeing little service in its final years ended the post-war reign of the P class at Stewarts Lane when it was withdrawn in February, 1960.

No. 31555 in British Railways 'sunshine' livery at Stewarts Lane on 27 August 1949. *H.C.Casserley*

No. 1558 at Stewarts Lane MPD against the familiar background of Hamptons repository, and still carrying Southern livery as late as 8 March 1952, which indeed it retained till 25 July 1953. No. 30793 *Sir Ontzlake* is the King Arthur class on the right. *H.C.Casserley*

No. 31557 shunts the CWS milk depot siding at Stewarts Lane on 27 February 1957.

R.C.Riley

No. 31558 has graduated to higher things as it shunts Pullman cars in the Longhedge carriage depot at the back of Stewarts Lane on 15 September 1957. *R.C.Riley*

Under British Railways ownership No. 1178 ran as s1178 from 6 March 1948 to 18 May 1951, seen here at Brighton MPD. *J.H.Aston*

Brighton

If Dover had been the sheet anchor of the class from its earliest days, Brighton was certainly the pivot of the P tanks following the Second World War where during the 1940s, 1557 and 1323 alternating with 1178, had been allocated for the Kingston Wharf duty, one engine to shunt at Shoreham, the other to act as coal pilot and spare. The latter was the first member of the class to be renumbered in the short-lived British Railways 's' prefix style, running as s1178 from 6 March, 1948, until 18 May, 1951. In that year it was replaced at Brighton by 31325 which itself had spent part of the summer of 1948 on Brighton shed, and it was this locomotive that really made the headlines during the declining years of the class with its aforementioned exploits in Hampshire in 1949 and 1950.

Back at Brighton in 1951, it shared the Kingston Wharf turn with 31556 where arrangements continued smoothly until one or other of the locomotives was called away for major overhaul. The result was usually a complicated temporary reshuffle involving several members of the class, and occasionally the B4s and Terriers with whom the P tank movements were so closely entwined. Such a situation occurred in March, 1956, when 31325 was overhauled in Brighton, not Ashford Works, and B4 30083 arrived from Eastleigh on 18 March to assist in the shunting at Kingston Wharf in its absence. Although not lacking in power, the B4 soon made itself unpopular owing to limitations in braking and coal capacity, and insufficient speed on the return journey to Brighton each evening, inconveniencing the passenger service.

When 31325 returned to duty, Brighton's other P, 31556, was despatched to Ashford Works, but it was hoped to receive another of the class to dispose of the unpopular 0-4-0T. This did not immediately materialise, and the B4 lingered on at Brighton. The reason for the delay was that 31027, sent from Ashford, had failed at St. Leonards, and 31178 which had just failed at Ridham was patched up as quickly as possible at Ashford and sent in lieu, arriving on 23 April. Meanwhile to everyone's relief, 30083 had departed for Eastleigh, and with the return on 31556 from Ashford after general overhaul on 4 May, the situation returned to normal.

Hayling Monopoly Broken

In May, 1957, 31325 was transferred for what was seemingly another spell at Eastleigh for the Winchester duty. Then came the amazing news that the age-old monopoly of the Brighton Terriers on the Hayling Island branch had been broken by the publication of authority for the ex-S.E.C.R. P class to run over this line, together with authorisation for use on the Lyme Regis line too. Shortage of Terriers may have been acute, for 31325 was reported to have anticipated this permission by working a trial trip on the Hayling Island branch during Whitsun week, possibly on tests to confirm the above authorisation. The small boiler of the P was not surprisingly found inadequate, and any idea of supplementing the Terriers was dropped.

The scene at Winchester City on 24 June 1957 with No. 31325 on a turn of duty. The one road one engine shed, a sub-depot to Eastleigh, is seen immediately behind the locomotive. In the platform given the right-away stands Standard 4MT 2-6-0 No. 76067 prepared to resume with a northbound stopping train.   *R.C.Riley*

Dieselisation

Meanwhile over at both Dover and Brighton the fate of the P tanks was threatened by imminent introduction of light 204 h.p. diesel mechanical locomotives ex-Drewry/R.S.H., of which 11220-6 were initially allocated at Hither Green and soon spread to every tiny corner of the Region for tests and duties hitherto worked by classes A1X, B4 and P, beginning with 11220 diagramed for a trial period on Stewarts Lane 78 duty, the Milk Depot shunter on 23 April, 1957. In the week commencing 6 May, the same locomotive worked a series of trials on the K.E.S.R. line, stabling at Robertsbridge, and then moved on to Dover shed, being tested in the Town Yard and Ferry Dock, and in July on the East Kent line trips between Shepherdswell and Tilmanstone. On 23 September it began regular work on the Dover Harbour Board lines to the Eastern Docks, being left overnight Mondays to Fridays under a street lamp at the Western Docks on a road to which the public had access, returning to shed at mid-day Saturday for the weekend.

On 12 May 11222 arrived at Brighton shed for instructional purposes, trials being made at Kingston Wharf and Newhaven Harbour with a view to displacing steam shunters. By the beginning of June it was in regular use on the Kingston Wharf shunting duty (No. 778), being accommodated in the transit shed at Shoreham overnight, and returning to Brighton fortnightly. On 8 August it went to Brighton to have adjustments made. 31556 was therefore sent to Kingston Wharf in lieu for the next two days, and continued to deputise on further occasions both there and in October, when no Terrier was available, on the duty at Littlehampton Quay, another L.B. & S.C.R. harbour flop where sidings had been laid down in the 1860s for sailings to the Channel Isles and Honfleur. Like Shoreham, the passenger steamers were soon withdrawn leaving a declining service for small cargo vessels which terminated in the mid-1960s.

In August, 1958, 31325 was recalled from Winchester when 11222 had to be sent to Eastleigh, and did a further stint at Shoreham. Subsequently, Doncaster built D2082, one of the latest batch of Drewry diesels, received damage in the course of its journey down from Hither Green to Brighton to take over the Kingston duty, and required repairs before it could be put into use, and this kept the Ps in business in March, 1959. During that year 31325 also acted as coal pilot on a number of occasions, and at least once deputised for a Terrier on the Works shunting duty, while 32670 got its own back by shunting Kingston Wharf on one occasion.

Final Withdrawals

But the end of service on the national system was in sight, and this was made abundantly clear in the 1960 Locomotive Condemnation Programme which indicated that all five remaining P tanks were to be taken out of service by 28 November, 1960, part of a deliberate policy by which P tanks were being sacrificed for Terriers, only one of the latter, 32677, being withdrawn that year. Not that the surviving Ps were in poor condition, for 31325 had gone through Ashford Works in August, 1958, while 31027 and 31556 had received casual repairs there in November 1959, and January, 1960, respectively.

However, unlike the Terriers still active at Hayling and Newhaven, all that the P class survivors could now hope for was occasional stand-by duties. The axe fell in February, 1960, when 31558 was withdrawn and cut up at Ashford with indecent haste in the week ending 20 February. 31325 from Brighton went the same way, being withdrawn in March and cut up during the week ending 26 March, while 31027 languished at the back of Dover shed.

31556 continued to hold the fort at Brighton, enjoying a final moment of glory when deputising on the Works shunting turn, for 32635 (formerly 377s) which had been derailed in Brighton shed. Shortage of Terriers could still be acute at times for on 21 May H class 31308 had to shunt Littlehampton Wharf. On 26 June 31323 paid a passing visit to Brighton on its way to a new destination but by then it had been sold out of service. 31027 lasted at Dover till March, 1961, and in a similar fashion spent the nights of 16 and 17 at Brighton shed, where 31556 still soldiered on until mid-June when it was seen, newly painted black with no visible signs of identity or ownership, awaiting despatch to its new home. The reign of just over half a century by the P tanks over the lightly laid and sharply curved by-ways of the national system came to an end on 14 June, 1961, when 31556 departed light engine from Brighton eastwards towards retirement in what proved to be familiar pastures.

Final Mileages

| 31027 | 523,282 | 31323 | 564,623 | 31555 | 422,212 | 31557 | 653,488 |
| 31178 | 516,165 | 31325 | 409,508 | 31556 | 473,563 | 31558 | 447,464 |

These figures are not quite complete. As previously noted, service in the R.O.D. does not appear to have been recorded, and in most cases the BR mileage between last overhaul and withdrawal has been omitted. No. 31323 is the only one with a complete repair and mileage history.

One of the last regular duties of the class was the Kingston Wharf shunt at Shoreham

Above: No. 31556 is seen on its way down from the connecting spur to the main Coast line which led to the quayfront.

Right: The harbourfront scene on the bright winter morning of 26 January 1959 as No. 31556 waits for some shunting to turn up.

Below: One month before withdrawal, No. 31325 brings a load of seaborne coal on 6 February 1960 up the grade to the main line, the shunter travelling on the footplate to continue his work in the transfer sidings seen in the right background, a sight to remember as the little schoolboy stares in wonderment.

Photos W.M.J.Jackson

A historic day as the first member of the class to be preserved steams light engine past Polegate 'A' Box on 26 June 1960. There is a glowing smile on the signalman's face!

S.C.Nash

Bluebell (formerly No. 31323) takes pride of place on 7 August 1960 as the official inaugural train on the Bluebell Railway takes position alongside the platform at Sheffield Park. An animated scene indeed with spectators even ensconced on the top of the platform awnings.

Photo courtesy Bernsen's International Press Service

Private Ownership and Preservation

Bluebell

Standard gauge preservation in the South had started with the Bluebell Railway Preservation Society which held its inaugural meeting on 15 March, 1959, and in just over a year had made such strides as to be able to envisage operating trains over the 4 ½ mile of single track between Sheffield Park and Bluebell Halt at Horsted Keynes in the latter part of the 1960 season. On 17 May a Stroudley Terrier (ex-L.B.S.C. 55 *Stepney*) had been delivered to the line amidst rousing acclaim from enthusiasts and media. In the run up to the inspection necessary to obtain a Light Railway Order, it was realised that, with no run-round at Bluebell Halt, a second engine for attaching at the other end of the train would need to be obtained quickly.

Thanks to the help and cooperation of British Railways, and especially Mr. Cobb, the Sales and Contracts Manager at Waterloo, P class 31323 from Dover was purchased and delivered to the line on 27 June. It was in first class condition after a mechanical check-over at Ashford, having run only 5274 miles since its previous general repair there in September, 1958. Repainted in black, fitted with a copper cap to its chimney, and bearing its old S.E.C.R. number 323 in large

figures on the side tanks, work lovingly undertaken by old hands at the Works who remembered its construction, the engine had run light via Polegate to Brighton on 26 June and continued, facing south, to Sheffield Park the following day to a rather quieter reception than that given the Terrier. Were the enthusiasts possibly disappointed to accept a locomotive of such unknown pedigree?

It worked several non-public services and works trains up the line, and finally took its bow at the historic Re-opening Day on 7 August, 1960, its front end providing the platform for B.R.P.S. Chairman John Leroy's address opening the line. Following this Mrs. Anthony Kimmins cracked a bottle of champagne over 323's buffer beam in christening it *Bluebell*, the name in yellow lettering on the side tanks with the number in smaller lettering transferred to the bunker sides. This limelight gave the locomotive a special and unique niche in the story of a great railway enterprise. It ran through the short season to 30 October when it shared a special members' train to the newly opened Freshfield Halt with *Baxter*. 15023 passengers had been carried, double the promoters' target, and a trading profit was made.

Scene at Sheffield Park typical of the short 1960 opening season as *Bluebell* shunts ex-LSWR coach No. 320, one of the pair owned by the line at that time, in the precincts of the station to the interest of a growing number of visitors.
Courtesy Industrial Rimmer Photography

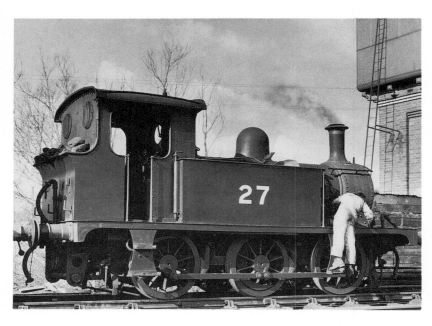

Left: No. 27, light engine, captured leaving the north portal of Clayton Tunnel bound for the Bluebell line on 18 March 1961.

W.M.J.Jackson

Right: Newly arrived at Sheffield Park, No. 27 receives a fitter's attention as it stands in light steam by the Pump House Siding.   *K.D.Chown*

Below: No. 27, about to lose its tank side number, stands out of steam at the entrance to the Woodyard Siding at Sheffield Park on 25 March 1961. In the far right distance there is a glimpse of the Terrier *Stepney.*   *R.C.Riley*

Primrose

The experience of the opening season made the purchase of a third passenger engine a top requirement in the Bluebell Railway's shopping list - "its spares to be interchangeable with *Stepney* or *Bluebell*." However the reply to the request for another Terrier from British Railways stated the latter would not be withdrawing another member of this veteran class for at least three years! So the Society in its urgent request for another operational locomotive before the commencement of the new season, came to be in negotiation for another P class locomotive.

Judging from the correspondence column in "Bluebell News", the idea of purchasing two of a class when so many other classes were in imminent danger of extinction, did not please everybody. But a second P it turned out to be, 31027, Dover's final member of the class, which entered Ashford Works for a brief visit in the course of which it was repainted and renumbered 27 in the same manner as the keen group of

S.E.C.R. stalwarts in the Works had done with 323. It ran light from Ashford to Brighton shed on 16 March, and two days later continued light under its own steam to Sheffield Park.

On 1st April, 1961, it was 27's turn to receive the sharp crack of a bottle of champagne, this time against its tank side, and to be christened *Primrose* (the name relating to the 'Bluebell and Primrose' line, the nickname for the upper part of the Lewes and East Grinstead Railway). The ceremony was conducted by the Bishop of Lewes, Geoffrey Warde, the newly elected President of the B.R.P.S.. who concluded his speech: -"I name this engine *Primrose*. May God bless those who drive and serve her, and all who travel on the Bluebell Line." Thus 27 became the first engine to be christened and blessed by a Bishop! Facing north, it took its place behind restored *Stepney* at the head of the newly-acquired Chesham set while *Bluebell* brought up the rear.

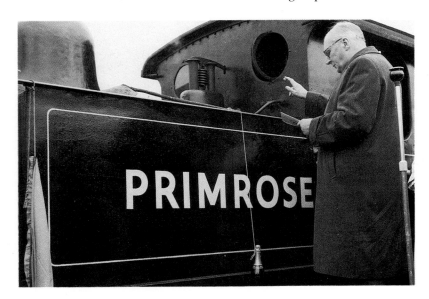

Naming ceremonies have been many, but the Bluebell Railway Preservation Society with its succession of presidential clergy actually blessed its locomotives! Bishop Warde of Lewes performs the ceremony on No. 27, now to be named *Primrose* at Sheffield Park on the first day of April, the opening day of the 1961 season.
K.D.Chown

Newly repainted *Primrose* stands at the ready at Sheffield Park with a working up the line in the spring of 1961.

Tom Martin

Bluebell and *Primrose*, back to back, make history together with *Stepney* and the Adams radial tank, with the set of four Ashbury Metropolitan coaches which formerly served the Chesham branch sandwiched between them, by becoming the first private railway to travel by right on British Railways track. The cavalcade has just entered Horsted Keynes with the 1.48 pm from Sheffield Park on 29 October 1961.

R.C.Riley

Bluebell attains stardom with Deborah Kerr, together with supporting staff of BRPS members on the occasion of the filming of 'The Innocents' during May 1961.   *BRPS Archives*

Bluebell stands at the makeshift Bluebell Halt at Horsted Keynes on 5 February 1962, having collected newly arrived rolling stock in the shape of DS 3208, an ex-SECR Birdcage Brake, and DS873, an ex-LCDR six wheeler.   *M.J.Mason*

On the Bluebell Railway

During that season a P at each end was a common feature of the services, and the pair formed part of a four-locomotive hauled train on 29 October, which was the first to resume running into the British Railways station at Horsted Keynes. Earlier in May *Bluebell* had figured large in the filming of "The Innocents" with Deborah Kerr, the first of an endless succession of shoots for anything from major films to brief television advertisements.

The 1962 season saw the first large scale maintenance carried out at Sheffield Park. Though all schedules were met without loss of running time, the Locomotive department was not without its maintenance problems. However with five available locomotives it was possible to ring the changes. *Primrose* received a partial retube, eight boiler tubes being renewed, and, soon after returning to service, it was *Bluebell's* turn to be laid up. The heavy peak traffic workings of the first two seasons were beginning to take toll of the motion work, wear fortunately being restricted to the big end bearings, and these were successfully taken up. Attention was also given to the brake blocks and, after skimming, rehanging and adjustment, 323 was outshopped. Both P tanks were available for another four-engine effort hauling the "Victory Belle" of 21 October over Bluebell metals.

1963 opened with 27 losing its name *Primrose* but splendidly restored to its original S.E.C.R. livery, complete with brass numbers, Ashford Works plates and a pair of magnificent Company crests. This was what locomotive restoration was all about. It developed injector trouble on the occasion of the "Spring Belle" whose arrival heralded the start of another running season. It was fitted with a new vacuum exhaust, ready to be unveiled by Mrs. Kimmins, deputising for her husband who was indisposed, on 26 May for all to see the full pristine glory of its original livery of dark Brunswick green upon the reddish-brown frames, edged out with yellow, light green and red trimmings, the work of Mr. Eric Edwards to whom tribute was paid. Yet another bottle of champagne was broken over the locomotive which was immediately pressed into service heading the ex-L.N.W.R. Observation Car and rake of five Bulleid coaches on loan during the absence of the Chesham coaches at the Metropolitan Centenary. During the season 27 was naturally much sought after by photographers, and not surprisingly it formed the regular locomotive inset to the 1963 front cover of "Bluebell News" as 323 had done in 1961.

The latter had required motion work attention consisting of reducing the big and little ends, but opened the 1963 season, though subsequently was taken out for a boiler inspection. On the closing day, 27 October, 323 was in charge of the regular service train, interchanging with the "Lancing Belle", the final train over the Ardingly link line. On the opening afternoon of the 1964 season, 21 March, it was 27's turn, carrying a commemorative headboard marking the first day of public running into the Up road of the former Lewes platform at Horsted Keynes. During the season both engines received minor attentions, 323 recalibration of steam and vacuum gauges, 27 adjustment to motion work and one tube replaced. The latter figured with 473 on the "Christmas Belle" special. The year ended with Bill Brophy, a regular driver, later to be the Bluebell's running shed superintendent, admitting that he had quickly grown attached to the P tanks and 27 in particular, and that the pair were continually trying to prove to each other their individual merits.

1965 opened with 27 hauling the Observation Car and two coaches, and over Easter double-heading with the Adams Radial 488. It fell to *Bluebell* with *Stepney* to enact the 5th Anniversary Special on 8 August. At the end of the season 323 was withdrawn for servicing, and the following spring given a complete repaint. Bluebell Sunday, 4 September, 1966, was 323's coming out day, becoming the first and only locomotive to date to wear the Railway's own livery of bluebell blue, lined with light blue, black, white and red. It carried an original set of oval work plates from withdrawn H tanks "Constructed at Ashford Works S.E. & C.R.", the other of two pairs presented for the P's by Mr. R. C. Riley, being fixed below the cabside window close to the side tanks. On the side below the coal bunker was a slightly larger oval number plate with the words "Bluebell" and "Railway" sandwiching the 323, a set specially struck for the engine. It also carried a distinctive brass whistle commandeered from a withdrawn B.R. Standard Class 5 4-6-0. The nameplates failed to arrive in time, but Eric Edwards painted on the names most attractively. Evading a downpour of rain, the unveiling ceremony was conducted by "Mr. Pastry", the comedian Richard Hearne, who called 323 "a dear old friend. I name this young lady *Bluebell*. God bless all who run in her." The Special then steamed away from Sheffield Park carrying incidentally the Bluebell Railway's millionth passenger.

Following that big day 323 was immediately taken out of service for retubing, as was 27 which had but 15 days duty and 3 standby turns that season. In 1967 323 returned to regular service on 9 June, double-heading on Sundays and Bank holidays due to non-availability of larger engines, and in the course of the season worked 58 turns and 2 standbys. On 17 September it was withdrawn for attention to its firebox, the inspector agreeing to the defects being welded and then, subject to a further inspection being favourable, returned to traffic.

The brunt of the carrying the burden of the previous six seasons was beginning to take its toll, and both P tanks were found to be wasting badly at the rear bottom of the outer fireboxes. Repairs and retubing on 27 commenced on 29 October, boiler tubes having to be cut to the correct length by the repair staff at the one room workshop beside the single road running shed at Sheffield Park. It received its hydraulic boiler test on 23 April, 1968, was steamed for testing purposes the following two week-ends, at which it showed a tendency to run hot. However, it returned to revenue-earning service on the "Blue Belle" on 12 May, and was reported hauling the former L.C.D.R. six-wheeler on a weedkilling train on 23 June. 323 had also returned to traffic, but remained on light duties for the early part of the season until new little end blocks had been delivered. Late in July, 27 suffered a cracked main frame, but was welded up and returned to service. Both P's were rostered (with 473) for the Line Purchase celebrations on 27 October, and double-headed the 3.30 p.m. to Horsted Keynes.

The Locomotive Department reported at the close of 1968:- "Looking back we ought to be grateful to our small engines and those responsible for getting them. 27 came to us because no Terrier was available at the time. How little coal these tiny 0-6-0Ts consume compared to *Birch Grove* and our other larger locomotives, how economically and adequately they handle the mid-week and Saturday traffic and often manage the heavy Sunday trains in tandem." The P tanks were at last beginning to be appreciated". Designed for light railway work, they had at last come into their own.

Above: The shortlived Holywell (Waterworks) Halt, opened by the famous Dr. Beeching on the first day of April 1962, welcomes an Up train hauled by No. 27 *Primrose* in charge of the Chesham set. The station had to close a season later because of traffic congestion caused by visitors' car parking by the narrow confines of the road underbridge.   *R.C.Riley*

Below: During the spring of 1963, No. 27 was painstakingly restored to full Wainwright livery including brass numerals and the ornate Company crest, and put straight into service following an unveiling ceremony on 26 May. Behind the former ex-LNWR Observation Coach are five of the six Bulleid coaches on loan during the absence of the Chesham set at the Metropolitan Centenery celebrations at Neasden.   *R.C.Riley*

Bluebell at the north end of Horsted Keynes on 27 October 1963 in the course of shunting the 'Brighton Bluebelle' comprising the six coach 'Lancing Belle' works set up towards the Leamland bridge in order to regain the platform for Ardingly and a return to Brighton. It was the final passenger train to run over the link line to Haywards Heath. No. 55 *Stepney* and No. 473 *Birch Grove* at the far end, once released, will run round to the front.
Christine Riley

During the spring of 1966 *Bluebell* was returned to traffic in the Railway's own livery of bluebell blue, lined with light blue, black, white and red, and the name painted in nameplate fashion on the tank sides. It is seen entering Sheffield Park on a winter season one-coach working.
D.M.C.Hepburne-Scott

The Bluebell's prestige train of the afternoon, the 'Wealden Rambler', is taken up towards Freshfield in fine style by No. 27 and No. 473 *Birch Grove*.
D.M.C.Hepburne-Scott

In the early seventies *Bluebell* received a proper cast nameplate together with the Company's own crest and motto - 'Floreat Vapor' - 'May Steam Flourish!' It is seen at Sheffield Park with a machinery train on 5 April 1973.

Ian De Maid

No longer sporting its crest, *Bluebell* takes up the first train of the day, a photogenic goods for the benefit of photographers on 31 July 1977. The load here consists of a milk tank, more recently filled with water and used on the Railway's Fire Train, and a Guards van from the former Longmoor Military Railway. *Brian Stephenson*

Service in the 'Seventies

Unfortunately incomplete records of workings and mileages were kept prior to 1969, though the preceding paragraphs give a good idea of the role of the P tanks over that period. However, painstaking records by Bill Brophy and the Bluebell Railway Locomotive Department over the next decade has produced the following table of mileage statistics which highlights at a glance the tremendous contribution made by the pair of humble P tanks.

	27	323	Total Seasonal Miles
1969	3305(2)	7021(1)	14957
1970	4005(2)	4500(1)	13339
1971	5238(1)	3862(2)	12810
1972	2189(3)	4000(1)	12414
1973	1346(5)	2815(1)	12751
1974	2277(3)	-	12845
1975	-	-	
1976	-	-	
1977	-	1384(5)	13209
1978	-	1731(5)	13513
10yr Total	18360(2)*	25313(1)	

* The 3rd highest total mileage was 30064 with 14664 miles. Figures in brackets indicate position in individual locomotive mileage table.

Some explanation is required as to why by the end of 1973 the two (active) P tanks had seen their Indian summer pass. They had served the growing Bluebell Railway preservation venture almost non-stop since their arrival, and had been handling the majority of services, especially during the early period when an engine was required at each end. From the Mid-'sixties the Company had acquired locomotives of medium power like the Adams Radial tank, *Birch Grove*, and the "Dukedog" to haul the increasing traffic, now beyond the scope of a single P tank except on the lighter off-peak and winter workings at the less demanding ends of the season. The P's were used in pairs or double-heading with one of the larger engines as traffic increased yet further.

The early 1970's saw the arrival of still heavier motive power like the B.R. Standard Class 4 and *Blackmore Vale*, but it was some years before these were rendered available for traffic, and the P's soldiered on till by 1975 both were in need of a major overhaul. Fortunately by this date plans for the new Locomotive Works at Sheffield Park were already underway and soon in being, and *Bluebell* was an early entry candidate. However the need for only one small locomotive for pilot duties left 27 and the Terriers well down the priority list of repairs, the Railway being more concerned to see in use the medium range of locomotives which by 1977 included fellow Wainwright C class 592 and H class 263, giving the stud very much a preponderant South-Eastern flavour.

The highlights and major service details of this ten year period are briefly as follows. 1969 and 1970 were busy seasons for both locomotives. 27 partook in some advertisement filming in March, 1970, and on the 10th Anniversary celebrations on 2 August the two P tanks did a re-enactment of the first train as *Stepney* was not available, double-heading the Special back to Sheffield Park. Boxing Day that year witnessed a handsome fall of snow with 27 much in photographic demand. 27 continued throughout the following season, doing much combined work with *Birch Grove*. Meanwhile the previous winter 323 was called in for extensive repairs including the fitting of a new bunker, and returned to traffic in the summer of 1971 carrying the Bluebell Railway's coat of arms and motto "Floreat Vapor" on a beautiful crest on the side tanks, once again the meticulous work of Eric Edwards. It was used on 2 January, 1972, to haul the Wedding Special of Driver Tom Dobson, later to become a Bluebell Director, and snow graced the picturesque occasion yet again.

The P tanks continued through the 1972 season, 323 getting involved in some advertising for whisky on 26 July. Early in 1973 both were due for an external boiler examination, and entered the season late. 323 was withdrawn from traffic in September, leaving 27 to soldier on in 1974. It was seen frequently on the early goods working on High Days, and was heavily involved in Parade Day activities on 12 May. At the end of the height of the season it too succumbed and has since remained out of traffic awaiting a general overhaul estimated in 1976 as costing £14,000. A reboilering was planned for 323 whose parts were to be seen at the time "scattered in piles all over the yard." The general overhaul started in 1976, quickly speeded up when the new Locomotive Works came into operation; *Bluebell* was the second locomotive to take up temporary residence there. It received a repaint and returned to traffic at the end of the year, since which time it became involved in much shunting round the locomotive yard, cramped for space as the new three-road running shed was being constructed. It was on regular pilot duties the next three seasons, after running the `10.52 a.m. Sunday goods up to Horsted Keynes in order to be up to shunt the necessary carriage sets required for the peak afternoon services.

It was also much in demand prior to Christmas for providing steam heating on the seasonal specials. It was working in blizzard conditions on New Year's Eve, and the first day of 1979 saw 323 in charge of skeleton services in another snowridden pastorale. Soon after it suffered a loose eccentric sheath requiring all the motion to be taken down, but it was back in steam to celebrate Bluebell Stamp Day, 21 March, 1979, hauling the Travelling Post Office coach with the editor of the *Stamp Magazine* on the footplate. The occasion was the issue of the 15p rail letter fee stamp which depicted *Bluebell*. On 14 May it was photographed on a Wiggins Teape special with the GNR saloon in tow. Over the year it was rostered most Sundays and Bank Holidays.

It was called in for winter maintenance, appeared in February/March in use for TV commercials and photography stills and came into regular traffic in Easter week 1980. This was to prove a memorable year for the engine. On 11 May, Parade Day, 323 was one of eight locomotives in steam and was involved in a lot of double heading. It received a routine boiler check at the end of May, and on 2 August performed on the 20th Anniversary special, titled 'The Pioneer', with *Fenchurch* up front as *Stepney* was not available. On 14 September, Vintage Sunday, it was paired with *Fenchurch* throughout the day. Four days later it was reported leaving Sheffield Park on a low loader!

Bluebell on the East Somerset Railway

Following negotiations between the East Somerset and Bluebell Railway Companies the outcome was the transfer on 18 September 1980 of *Bluebell*, for twenty years the diminutive flagship of the line. Displaying the livery and crests of its namesake railway, it was winched onto a transporter with a little help from the Adams radial and by mid-afternoon was ready to begin its long journey west to Cranmore - in fact probably the longest journey that the engine had ever made. The trip went without incident and, after an overnight stop near Botley, 323 was unloaded at Foster Yeoman's quarry at East Cranmore to await tow by a Class 47 diesel up the branch, this taking place on 25 September.

The loan of 323 was to help relieve a motive power shortage on the ESR. It was steam tested on 28 September and, following a favourable mechanical examination, worked the 2.45 pm train to Merryfield Lane and back, double heading with Jinty 47493. It entered traffic officially on 4 October and operated until the end of the season when it was cleaned out, greased up and stored for the winter period.

It returned to service on 4 April 1981, in readiness for the first day's service on the morrow which saw the Jinty failed, and 323 handled the bulk of the train service alone. With the repaired Jinty and 9F 92203 *Black Prince*, it operated a successful Easter weekend, only to be snowed up by drifts seven days later. Between 24-26 May it received its annual boiler inspection and was back for the late Spring Bank Holiday weekend, and shared with Austerity 0-6-0ST 68005 the annual Schools Days, 9-12 June.

Bluebell was involved in high drama that winter. It handled the first ever ESR Santa Specials on 6 December, but the following weekend after a night of sub-zero temperatures 323 was preparing to leave with the 11.45 am train with 32 passengers on board when a sudden and violent blizzard erupted which quickly covered the track with snow. *Lord Fisher* was commandeered from an Engineer's train and summoned to assist *Bluebell* on the now thirty minute late special. The journey back was even more hazardous with visibility down to less than 15 yards and snow blowing horizontally through the cab, burning the faces of the crew. Soon after, the line was confirmed as blocked by snowdrifts. In the shed yard, in the time that it took to uncouple 323 from the train, drifting snow built up so rapidly around its wheels to a height of almost two feet that the crew literally had to dig the engine out to get it back into the shed. Raging winds damaged three of the large shed doors, and nine members of the ESR staff were marooned at the depot as all roads were impassable.

The final weekend of the year closed on a quieter note. *Bluebell* had been steamed 38 times in 1981, and was to record 27 days in operation in 1982 and 30 in 1983. It resumed its routine life that following spring, taking a generous share of the passenger workings. The five minute jaunt hauling usually two coaches along the easy graded stretch to Merryfield Lane was hardly a taxing proposition in normal circumstances. The visitor won the quiet and ungrudging respect of the Cranmore engine crews.

The following year 323 participated in an Enthusiasts' weekend, 8/9 October, when a number of goods trains were bravely diagramed into the service for the benefit of photographers, and 323 ran a couple of these turns. With the larger engines again in use, 323 acted as yard pilot on Sundays. It was working the December Santa trains when it developed leaking boiler tubes. Frantic efforts were made to replace the defective tubes only to discover more were leaking. Clearly the problem was going to become unending as the tubes were becoming due for a complete replacement. A return to its parent railway was very much on the cards.

In good company at Cranmore shed coupled to Jinty 0-6-0T No. 47493. Other locomotives on view are Class 9F 2-10-0 No. 92203 *Black Prince*, Austerity 0-6-0ST No. 68005 and one of the Doxford crane tanks. The occasion was an Enthusiasts' Day on the ESR on 20 September 1981.   *Rex Coffin*

On loan to the East Somerset Railway, *Bluebell* approaches Merryfield Lane on 28 June 1981.
J.W.T.House

Necessary attention and check up follows No. 323's return from Somerset. A place is found in the new Locomotive Works at Sheffield Park alongside the Wainwright C class 0-6-0 No. 592.
Mike Esau

Bluebell takes the 2.30 pm Buffet working up the grades past Tremaines through the winter snowscene on 10 February 1985.
A.Eaton

End of a Chapter?

323 returned to Bluebell metals during the third week of May 1984. Following retubing, repainting and hydraulic testing, it reentered service in early September to remain in traffic throughout to the close of the season. On 3 November it double headed with the North London tank a special celebration party for the commissioning of Sheffield Park's new inner home signal. It was one of eight locomotives on parade on 11 May 1985, and on 13/14 July participated in the Cavalcade of Steam weekend to good effect. It was called in to help *Stepney* up the line due to the latter's boiler starting the day containing no water and showing little water in the glass by the time it was coupled to its scheduled train. Late in the day it stepped in for the North London tank held up at Horsted over a suspicious knock in the right side cylinder.

The Railway's 25th Anniversary fell on 7 August, and the 1960 two coach special was re-enacted using the two original engines, *Stepney* leading and *Bluebell* trailing. Only coach 320 was not available, 1098 substituting. 323 was out of service during the winter awaiting repairs to its firebox and was taken into the Works during April 1986. A closer inspection of the firebox revealed problems with the outer wrapper, and as a result the firebox was condemned. 'The locomotive is therefore out of service awaiting boiler repairs', appeared to be the final line for some time.

Mileages for 323

1979	1578	1983	221(ESR)
1980	724	1984	752
1981	Not recorded est. 300	1985	1063
1982	168(ESR)		

However, to everyone's surprise *Bluebell's* lay-off was shortlived for in November, 1989, it entered the Works. It was intended that when heavy boiler repairs had been carried out, 323 would be available for the proposed Northern Extension shuttle service. This was passed for train services as far as Horsted House Farm on 13 April 1990, and *Bluebell* was duly there to keep its appointment, and continued to work 'The Extension Pioneer' through the season.

Pioneer II

The saga might well have stopped there but for the fact that two other survivors of this now famed class were waiting in the wings for their moment to arrive. Back in June, 1958, 31178 had been sold out of service to Bowaters of Sittingbourne for use on their standard gauge sidings. For many years the Company, then Edward Lloyd Ltd., did not own a standard gauge locomotive, shunting being carried out by a S.E.C.R. (later Southern Railway) engine as required. In 1936 the firm bought its first standard gauge engine from Bagnall (No. 2452). This was a 0-4-0ST and was named *Jubilee*. In view of its shunting close to the paper mills it featured spark arresting equipment inside the smokebox. After a period in 1970 as a reserve in case of failure of the ex-B.R. diesels which had been obtained, it was sold by Bowaters in 1971.

In 1943 a spare standard gauge 0-4-0ST was obtained secondhand from Messrs. Smith, Patterson & Co. Ltd of Blaydon. It carried plates showing that it had been rebuilt by Hudswell, Clarke & Co. in 1906, and was originally built in 1885 by Manning Wardle as No. 942. It was named *Pioneer*. It was only to be used when *Jubilee* was laid up for repairs, but on several occasions both were laid up together so that a

Southern Railway engine had to be borrowed, in July, 1944, for instance R1 class 0-4-4T 1699, on another apparently the small 0-4-0ST 3458 *Ironside*. *Pioneer* seems to have done very little work, and was scrapped in 1954.

The fill-in visits of 31178 in 1953, and again early in 1956, and of 32670 later that year have been described previously. The P returned to Ridham in 1958, not as a 'guest' this time but as a member of the family, having been purchased by Bowaters after its withdrawal by British Railways in June. On arrival at Ridham it was completely stripped down for a full overhaul. It was repainted to an approximation of its original S.E.C.R. livery of dark green panelled in pale green, and named *Pioneer II* (always referred to as "Pioneer the Second", not "Pioneer Two"). The name was painted centrally on the side tanks in a pleasing style of semi-italic block capitals. It was the only locomotive owned by either Lloyds or Bowaters that did not carry a brass nameplate.

In February, 1969, a standard gauge diesel locomotive was bought from British Railways, diesel mechanical D2259 (Drewry/RSH 11229), followed in July by D2228 (Drewry/Vulcan 11134), members of the very type of engine that had given the P class their final push from their dockland strongholds. That same year Bowaters planned that their own railway operation would cease in the autumn, and on Saturday, 4 October, 1969, a "last day" ceremony was arranged at Kemsley Mill at which the deeds of the Sittingbourne and Kemsley Light Railway were handed over by Bowaters to the Locomotive Club of Great Britain.

Early in 1969 it was found that the P tank had suffered cylinder damage of sufficient magnitude to make it uneconomical to carry out repairs and it was withdrawn from service, standing derelict at Kemsley Mill for several weeks. It was then given a superficial cleaning and put on display with the two aforementioned diesels. Replacement road vehicles had not arrived in sufficient quantities, and a few trains continued to operate until 26 October.

At that time *Pioneer II* had been destined for the Kemsley Down museum as a static exhibit. Learning that this locomotive was stored out of use, the Bluebell Railway management agreed an approach should be made to Bowaters, intimating that it could maintain the locomotive in working order. After some very quick negotiations following an inspection by members of the Bluebell's Locomotive department, it was sold and removed to Sheffield Park on 14 October, arriving with some useful spare parts accompanied by a valuable spare boiler. *Bluebell News* reported: "It will not run for a while, however, as it has a hole in its cylinders." A truer word was never written, but contrary to some premises it was not to be cannibalised to keep the other two Bluebell members of the class alive. It was fully intended eventually to restore this locomotive to traffic, and meanwhile, to render it an acceptable static exhibit, it was repainted in 1975 to Southern black livery with "Southern" above 1178 in large straw lettering on the tank sides.

So it remained in different corners of the various sidings at Sheffield Park until 1989, when an approach was made from a group within the Port Line project to purchase, restore and return 1178 to the line in working order. The question of motivation was central to its future restoration, and it was felt a group both designated and, as a result, dedicated to the locomotive would generate the means, money and manpower to accomplish its restoration. The restoration team at Sheffield Park expect few problems as it is largely complete and its main components known quantities. When restored 1178 will remain based at the Bluebell but will be available to visit other lines. There is every prospect of a return to steam in the early 1990s for the only member of the surviving quartet not to have been restored to active service so far in preservation.

Above: Photographs of *Pioneer II* (alias No. 31178) actually moving in steam are rare indeed. The veteran P tank returns to base at Ridham Dock at the end of a turn of duty. A brave attempt has been made to imitate Wainwright's original livery but it is only an approximation.　　*A.Muckley*

Right: Pioneer II sports an ungainly extension to its chimney, a very basic spark arrester necessary in view of shunting at Bowaters Paper Mills. This photograph affords a rare view of part of the standard gauge engine shed at Ridham Dock.　　*P. Winding*

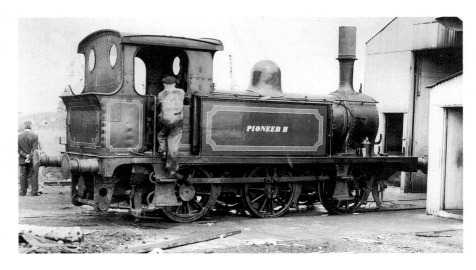

Below: The end is near for the pair of locomotives used to shunt the Bowater Lloyds standard gauge exchange sidings at Ridham. The 0-4-0T *Jubilee* and *Pioneer II* are lined up out of steam by the shed for photographers on 30 July 1968.
　　P.H.Groom

Purchased from Bowaters in 1969, the former No. 31178 spent the next twenty years standing around out of use in the yard at Sheffield Park. In 1975 it was decided to give it a facelift and superficial paint to Southern black livery with large straw coloured lettering. It is seen here in the old shed extension in company with the ex-North London dock tank No. 2650 and West Country Pacific No. 21C123 *Blackmore Vale.*

P.Winding

Pride of Sussex

The fourth and final survivor was last described steaming eastwards from Brighton on 14 June, 1961, with some urgency. This came about because of the closure of the Robertsbridge-Tenterden section of the former Kent and East Sussex Railway. The ultimate passenger working was a seven-coach enthusiasts' excursion on 11 June, but the line was by no means clear of wagons, and further trips up the branch took place the following week. A Preservation Society had been called into being at Northiam on 13 May, but most anxious and urgent of all was the proprietor of the Robertsbridge flour mills at North Bridge Street (between Robertsbridge and Salehurst Halt). Determined that his premises should remain rail-connected, Mr. Thomas Dadswell had been completing negotiations for a small locomotive with which to work his traffic to and from Robertsbridge station.

British Railways came up with their last P tank and, following a favourable inspection at Brighton, 31556 two days later became the property of James Hodson and Sons Ltd of Robertsbridge, appropriately returning to Kent and East Sussex metals again to be used the following day by Hodsons to transport their grain along the remaining active stub to and from the main Hastings line. Like *Pioneer II* the locomotive was repainted in a form of SECR green livery but *Pride of Sussex*, the name bestowed upon it, though in literal sense an apposite one, was in fact a regional brand of flour which, advertised across the side tanks in the form of a large scroll with a small shield with its six Sussex martlets below,

was rather overdone. Purchase of the engine provided justification for the rail connection to be kept, the line to the sidings being maintained by BR, thus facilitating the continued use of bulk grain wagons from Avonmouth Docks as well as fertilisers from Fisons and ICI. The engine was steamed four or five times weekly and was operated by the relatively inexperienced mill staff without any mishap. Some fairly heavy boiler and firebox repairs were carried out on site in order to maintain its service, and it was run in on the section of line up towards Salehurst. The Mill Manager was a keen enthusiast and often drove the locomotive around the sidings himself.

But by 1965 the engine was described as "presenting a rather forlorn appearance and needs some mechanical attention if she is to give reliable service much longer." Indeed it saw little service after the mid-'sixties for urgent work was needed again on the firebox. On a number of occasions a Terrier, either former partner 32670, soon again to become No. 3 *Bodiam*, or 32650 which was named *Sutton* after the London borough which adopted it, and later in 1967 a diesel from Ford's Works, Dagenham, were hired to the mill owners by the Kent and East Sussex Railway Preservation Society, which had been formed in 1961 to rescue the line and had collected several locomotives at Rolvenden for eventual use on it. In fact, the Society provided not only a locomotive but a driver to boot on many occasions.

A rare photograph of *Pride of Sussex* (formerly No. 31556) out at work on the former Kent and East Sussex line, seen on 18 June 1965 bring a trainload of grain hoppers round the curve from Robertsbridge towards Hodsons Mill.

Tim Stephens

Pride of Sussex displaying its shield of Sussex martlets stands out of steam at Hodsons Robertsbridge flour mills on 7 April 1967, its turns of duty taken over by the ex-Fords Works diesel locomotive seen in the right background.

C.Shaw collection

Into Preservation

Early in 1969 the flour side was closed down in order to concentrate on animal feedstuffs, and in September Hodsons decided that they had no further use for *Pride of Sussex*. The siding was officially closed on 1 January, 1970, after having served the mill for some 66 years. Despite stiff competition from the Bluebell Railway, it was acquired for use on the Kent and East Sussex, being transferred to Rolvenden by road in January, 1971. *Pride of Sussex* was found to be in need of extensive repairs, was given a priority overhaul, renumbered and became their No. 11 and eventually steamed once or twice in Rolvenden yard. As reported in *The Farmers' Line* for Autumn 1972: 'The major overhaul of P class 0-6-0T No. 11 is complete at long last, and after a satisfactory steam test in July, the locomotive moved under its own steam for the first time for many years on 13 August. In the Co's fully lined out green livery with cast number-plates, the locomotive is a great credit to all who worked on her.' The boiler, however, had to be removed in April, 1974, and was sent to the Medway College of Technology where the firebox stays were removed and wasted plates replaced, returning in September, 1975. Early in 1976 the wheels were sent to British Rail, Ashford, for turning. However, due to financial restraints and shortages of labour, *Pride of Sussex* was unlikely to return to service for quite some time. Welding work remained to be done on the boiler, the tubes needed replacing and the boiler

mountings overhauling. The main frames of the locomotive stood on packing at Rolvenden, awaiting boring of the axle boxes, refitting of the slide bars, provision of new piston rods and the obtaining of a new piston head.

Some attention was given in 1977 to tapping out stay holes and fitting studs and boiler mountings, but the following year 'work on the boiler was progressing slowly'! There was the prospect of lining up the frames in 1980; the firebox stays arrived that summer, but shortage of time and manpower saw no work done on the 'P' for some time. Meanwhile three axlebox keeps were made to replace those stolen several years previously. In 1983 six keep retaining pins were manufactured and new axlebox oil pads found, while casting of new piston heads was farmed to an outside contractor. During the next year there was further attention to repairs on the boiler, but thereafter the work was reported as having slowed down yet again: - 'Priority of labour and time is devoted to running trains and maintaining locomotives in traffic'. By the end of 1985 the slide bars were in place, the crossheads were due for completion and the frame was taken for a slow trundle along the line to check that all was well. By the spring of 1986 the boiler had passed its hydraulic test, safely installed between the frames. Attention to the tanks followed, and by May the locomotive was in undercoat prior to painting in early BR livery as 31556.

The first attempt at restoration appeared creditable on the surface, but *Pride of Sussex* in the new KESR green livery, with the boiler in poor condition, was once again dismantled in 1974.
Photo courtesy Tenterden Railway Co.

Return to Service

Freshly outshopped, it entered traffic on 30 November, 1986, and operated a couple of two-coach trial trips, scaling Tenterden bank unassisted despite adverse weather conditions, confirming two coaches as its declared load limit when working trains on its own. The following month it double-headed several Santa Specials, and during the winter close-down it powered a number of works trains, recording a mileage of 336 in its first month in service. In the close season it lost its BR running number and served for a while in plain black. On 5 May, 1987, it featured in a sales promotion event for Mercedes cars, and at the end of June attended Gravesham Edwardian Fair at Gravesend on a low loader. In July it was turned out as 1556 in the Southern Railway livery of black with green lining out and yellow numbering and letters worn when it was first hired by the KESR in 1936. On 28 July it was formally returned to traffic by the Mayor of Ashford, its birthplace. In the 1987 season it did on several occasions tackle Tenterden bank solo with two coaches, but was more usually seen in company with *Charwelton*, often on Wealden Pullman workings. On several summer Sundays it filled in as Tenterden station pilot, having come up from Rolvenden hauling the midday goods train. Early in December it was temporarily withdrawn for its boiler examination as well as the fitting of a brick arch to improve steaming, reduce coal consumption and lessen spark emission. All the boiler tubes were beaded over. On 16 May, 1988, it featured on an ARPS Luncheon special paired with *Sutton* and on the evening Dinner train with *Charwelton*. 1556 had become very much part of the Kent and East Sussex scene it had first come to acquainted with more than half a century previously, the wheels having turned full circle! 1556 staked an even greater claim to fame when, on 23 July 1989, as part of the 'Challenge Anneka' exercise, it triumphantly hauled the historic first train into Northiam Station, a landmark in the bid by the KESR to return eventually to Bodiam.

The KESR's P tank first returned to service in 1986 back in its final BR livery as No. 31556, photographed double heading with Austerity 0-6-0ST No. 24 *William H. Austen* a Santa Special on its way to Wittersham Road on 13 December that year.

Brian Stephenson

To a great cheer from a large crowd of well wishers, No. 1556 steams across the A28 road to meet a deadline into Northiam on 23 July 1989, driven by veteran KESR driver Jack Hoad who had started on the independent light railway half a century previously.

Brian Stephenson

A Permanent New Role in Preservation

Enough has surely been said to underline the vital new role of the P tanks in preservation. A few final choice comments are worth recording in print. Terry Cole, a Chairman of the Bluebell Railway and an experienced driver, writes: - "It has been under Bluebell management that the hitherto obscure P class tanks have reached their zenith, proving themselves consistently free steaming, reliable and economic performers, and have clocked more train miles individually than any other of our engines." And to quote Bill Brophy yet again: - "The P tanks are now proven to be one of the finest preservation discoveries."

"Inexpensive to run, easy to maintain and reliable in service," is the general commendation from those who handle and run the survivors of the class in today's preservation field. From both footplate and maintenance personnel comes the convinced assertion that these locomotives, working side by side with Terriers, have proved more reliable and economical. Was it, when working on the SECR, that standards were more exacting? Or, as seems more likely, have the passing years' altered circumstances narrowed the unquestionable superiority of the Terriers? The P class, built just short of 40 years later are obviously far less worn and, being smaller in size, are proving more economical.

Be that as it may, the final comment from Bill Brophy is totally apt: "Someone remarking on their performance said they might well have been built for our Railway! He could not have said a truer word for light railway work was their designer's very intention."

Boilers

No spare boilers were built for the P class, and the mileage cards show no boiler changes occurring on any of these engines. The two P class boiler swaps that have taken place have been since BR withdrawal. Bowaters put the boiler off withdrawn 31557 onto 31178, and the latter's old boiler came with the locomotive to the Bluebell Railway which fitted it on 323 *Bluebell*.

No. 31027, now returned to its original wartime SECR number 27, overnights at Brighton shed on 17 March 1961 to receive minor mechanical attention before continuing on to join the Bluebell Railway.
Author's collection

Appendix I
Individual Histories

No.	Entered Traffic	'A' Prefix	Renumbering	1000 series	30000 series	Withdrawn	Disposal
27	2/10	10/26		4/36	6/48	3/61	Sold to Bluebell Railway Preservation Society
178	2/10	7/24		11/31	5/51 *	6/58	Sold to Bowaters & Lloyd Ltd. **
323	7/10	1/27		8/31	2/49	6/60	Sold to Bluebell Railway Preservation Society
325	7/10	7/24		6/37	1/49	3/60	Broken up at Ashford
555	6/10	10/26		4/38	5/48	2/55	Broken up at Ashford
753	2/09	-	A556 11/26	11/35	3/50	6/61	Sold to James Hodson & Sons Ltd. ***
754	2/09	1/24	A557 12/25	4/35	5/49	9/57	Broken up at Ashford
558	6/10	5/24		1/40	7/53	2/60	Broken up at Ashford

* Received temporary 'S' prefix 3/48.
** Resold to Bluebell Railway Preservation Society 10/69. Further sale to Port Line Project 4/89.
*** Resold to Kent and East Sussex Railway Preservation Society 10/69.

Appendix II
Allocations

No.	Entered Traffic	Allocation When New	July 1914	Jan 1917	Jan 1923	July 1928	July 1933	July 1937	Aug 1939	June 1945	May 1949	July 1953	Jan 1959
27	2/10	SHN	RDG	FOLK	FOLK	FOLK	FOLK	FOLK	FOLK	DOV	DOV	DOV	DOV
178	2/10	RDG	BAT	B.A	TON	FOLK	FOLK	FOLK	DOV	BRI	BRI	DOV	-
323	7/10	ORP	ORP	MARG	TON	FOLK	DOV	DOV	BRI	FOLK	FOLK	DOV	DOV
325	7/10	AFD	TON	AFD	HAST	FOLK	FOLK	FOLK	DOV	DOV	BRI	BRI	BRI
555	6/10	GILL	BAT	AFD	FOLK	BAT	DOV	DOV	FOLK	DOV	FOLK	BAT	-
753/556	2/09	TON	TON	BAT	AFD	BAT	FOLK	FOLK	FOLK	DOV	DOV	BRI	BRI
754/557	2/09	RDG	RDG	MARG	FOLK	FOLK	DOV	DOV	BRI	BRI	BRI	BAT	-
558	6/10	MARG	BAT	ORP	MARG	BAT	AFD	FOLK	FOLK	FOLK	FOLK	ELH	FOLK

AFD	Ashford	BAT	Battersea (Stewarts Lane)	B.A	Bricklayers Arms	BRI	Brighton
DOV	Dover	ELH	Eastleigh	FOLK	Folkestone	GILL	Gillingham (New Brompton)
HAST	Hastings	MARG	Margate	ORP	Orpington	RDG	Reading
SHN	Sheerness	TON	Tonbridge				

NB. From 1 September 1915 the SECR brought into use running shed distinguishing Numbers, when small white cast iron plates with red figures were fixed inside the cabs of all engines, usually on the driver's side.

Bibliography

Archives

Bluebell Railway Preservation Society
Dover Harbour Board
National Railway Museum, York
Public Record Office, Kew

Locomotive History

Minutes of the Locomotive, Carriage and Wagon Committee of the SE&CR (PRO)
D. L . Bradley - The Locomotive History of the South Eastern & Chatham Railway (RCTS)
F. Burtt - SE&CR Locomotives (Ian Allan Ltd)
K.Marx - Wainwright and his Locomotives (Ian Allan Ltd)
O.S.Nock - The Locomotives of R.E.L.Maunsell (Edward Everard)
W.G.Tilling - The Locomotives of the Southern Railway (Eastern Section)
N.Wakeman - SE&CR Locomotive List (Oakwood Press)

Company and Line Histories

Minutes of the Management Committee of the SER and LCD Railways
E.Course - The Railways of Southern England: Secondary and Branch Lines (Batsford)
E.Course - The Railways of Southern England: Independent and Light Railways (Batsford)
D. Gould - Westerham Valley Railway (Oakwood Press)
D. Gould - The South Eastern and Chatham Railway in the 1914-18 War (Oakwood Press)
R. M. Lyne - Military Railways in Kent (North Kent Books)
O. S. Nock - The South Eastern and Chatham Railway (Ian Allan Ltd)
H. P. White - A Regional History of the Railways of Great Britain Volume 2 - Southern England (Phoenix)
H. P. White - Forgotten Railways: South-East England (David & Charles)

Railway Journals

Bluebell News
Railway and Travel Monthly
Railway Magazine
Railway Observer
Southern Railway Magazine
The Tenterden Terrier

Acknowledgements

With special appreciation to the staff of Dover Harbour Board, Kent County Library, Ashford, the National Railway Museum, York, and the Public Record Office, Kew, for assistance given, and to Peter Cooper, Alan Gosling, Roger Hardingham, Dick Riley, Philip Shaw, Brian Stephenson and Peter Winding for many helpful and constructive comments during the writing and production of this locomotive class history, together with all those photographers whose work is reproduced in the pages that follow.

© Klaus Marx &
Runpast Publishing
1990
ISBN 1 870754 14 X

Typeset by
P.P.S Desktop Publishing Bureau
11 Holtham Avenue
Churchdown
Glos

Printed by
Doveton Press Ltd
Willway Street
Bedminster
Bristol